The historical geography of the clans of Scotland – Primary Source Edition

James Alexander Robertson, T B. 1813?-1897 Johnston

THE

HISTORICAL GEOGRAPHY

OF THE

CLANS OF SCOTLAND.

BY

T B JOHNSTON, F.R.G.S F.R.S.E & F.S.A.S.,

AND

Colonel JAMES A ROBERTSON, F.S.A.S

SECOND EDITION

W. & A. K. JOHNSTON,

GEOGRAPHERS, ENGRAVERS, AND PRINTERS TO THE QUEEN,

EDINBURGH AND LONDON

1873.

CONTENTS.

MAP OF SCOTLAND DIVIDED INTO CLANS,   FRONTISPIECE

PREFACE,   5

EXPLANATORY REMARKS ON THE MAP,   7

ROLL OF THE LANDISLORDIS AND BAILLIES,   8

ROTATION OF THE HIGHLAND CLANS AS GIVEN IN TWO ACTS OF PARLIAMENT, DATED 1587
AND 1594,   11

NAMES OF HIGHLAND CHIEFS AND LANDLORDS CONTAINED IN THE ACT OF PARLIAMENT 1587,
NOT NAMED IN THE ROLL OF THE CLANS,   13

STRENGTH OF THE HIGHLAND FORCES IN 1715,   13

BADGES OF THE CLANS,   14

WAR CRIES OF THE CLANS,   15

ITINERARY OF PRINCE CHARLES FROM HIS LANDING TO EDINBURGH,   16

ITINERARY OF PRINCE CHARLES FROM EDINBURGH TO CULLODEN,   17

ITINERARY OF PRINCE CHARLES FROM CULLODEN TO ARASAIG,   21

MAP OF THE VARIOUS ROUTES (TWO PAGES)

ACCOUNT OF THE BATTLE OF PRESTONPANS,   22

PLAN OF THE BATTLE

ACCOUNT OF THE BATTLE OF FALKIRK,   24

PLAN OF THE BATTLE.

ACCOUNT OF THE BATTLE OF CULLODEN,   26

MAP OF THE DISTRICT, WITH LINE OF MARCH OF THE TWO ARMIES

PLAN OF THE BATTLE

ACT OF PARLIAMENT, DATED 1746, FOR DISARMING THE HIGHLANDS, AND RESTRAINING THE USE
OF THE HIGHLAND DRESS,   30

Preface to the First Edition.

———

THE following publication was suggested by the frequent applications made to the Publishers for information as to the limits and positions of the districts occupied by the CLANS of SCOTLAND, and as to the correct line of separation between the Highlands and the Lowlands At first nothing more was intended than a reproduction of one of the old maps, which have now become scarce, but a little investigation showed that the best of them were very imperfect and inaccurate, and not worth reproducing In these circumstances it was found necessary to commence the work from the beginning, taking as a basis the Acts of Parliament of 1587 and 1594, for the reason given in the note explanatory of the Map After having produced the Map, it was thought that some interesting additions could be made to the publication, by combining with it, in a convenient form, several articles connected with the Highlands not of easy access to the general public,—such as the Roll of the Clans, Strength of the Highland Forces, their War Cries, Badges, etc Having gone so far, it followed almost as a matter of course, to introduce the last appearance of the Clans as an Army, when they rallied round the standard of the unfortunate Prince Charles, an interest in whose adventures, and those of his gallant followers, can never cease to be felt so long as the exquisite songs and ballads in which they are narrated, maintain their place as 'household words,' not only in every house in this country, but also in every distant land in which the Scottish emigrant has found a home This led to the Map of the Prince's Wanderings, the Plans and Descriptions of his Battles, and as a sequel, the Act of Parliament of 1746 for disarming the Highlands and restricting the Use of the Highland Dress

It will thus be seen that the work is not in any sense a history of the Clans, although, it is hoped, that it may be found a useful companion to any history of Scotland, or of the Highlands

Thanks are due to W F SKENE, LL D, for his very valuable assistance in laying down the Highland boundary which represents the traditional line, formed by the natural features of the country, whilst the limits of the respective clans, as coloured on the Map, represent the territory acquired by many of them beyond that line ; to JAMES DRUMMOND, R S A , for the use of his rare print of Culloden, from which the plan of the battle is compiled ; to DAVID LAING, LL D., and JOHN STUART, LL D , for valuable information and assistance

August 1872

———

Preface to the Second Edition.

———

THE call for a Second Edition of this work within a year, is a proof that the Publishers were not mistaken in supposing that it was required As might have been expected, orders have been received from all the colonies to which Highlanders have emigrated,—Canada, Australia, New Zealand, and also from the United States of America.

Advantage has been taken in this edition to correct a few errors that existed in the first ; a new Plan of the Battle of Falkirk, corrected from local information, has been substituted for that formerly given, and the colouring of the large map has been greatly improved and rendered more distinct The Publishers refer with pleasure to the very favourable reviews received, extracts from which will be found at the end of the volume

June 1873

Explanatory Remarks on the Map.

THE map is constructed and coloured to show the situation and possessions of the Clans, as well as the properties of the Landlords, in the Highlands and Islands of Scotland

The former (the Clans) are all enumerated in two Acts of Parliament, dated 1587* and 1594 †

The names of the latter (the Landlords) are appended to the Act of 1587, thus the names and possessions of the two parties having possession of all the north of Scotland, rests on an authentic historical basis

This early date has been selected, because most of the inhabitants occupied the districts they had inherited from their forefathers, as it was not till a later date that the stronger clans began to oppress the weaker, and deprive them of their inheritance.

Every effort has been made to secure, as far as possible, perfect accuracy for this purpose public and private records and histories have been searched, and it has been the earnest desire of the compilers to divide the land with the strictest impartiality, and in accordance only with the evidence before them. As no properly authenticated map, showing the positions of the Highland Clans has ever been offered to the public, it is hoped that the present publication will supply the defect It is true that General Stuart, in his work on the Highlands, attempted to represent the possessions of the clans as at the period of 1745, but it is in many particulars most inaccurate thus a whole clan (the MacNabs) is not named in his map, whilst the extensive estates of the Campbells of Lochnell and Barcaldine are represented as belonging to the Stewarts of Appin In Perthshire, the large estates of Robertson of Lude and Faskally, as also parts of that of Strowan, are represented as the property of the Stewarts and the Duke of Athol

The map is a strong corroborative proof of the now generally recognised fact, that the comparatively insignificant Irish colony which settled in Argyleshire, never could have acquired the large and extensive territories which belonged to the Highlanders of Scotland, as it is impossible that this trifling colony could have dispossessed the original inhabitants of the country, the ancestors of the Gael of Alban, the descendants of the valiant Caledonians, and not of the Irish, as the fabulous writers have pretended

The rotation, and the numbering of the clans, have been made exactly [as they occur in the Acts of Parliament, so also is that of the landlords of the Highlands and Islands

On the map, the residences of the chiefs and those of the heads of families are marked in black, having the number of the clan below in *upright print*, while the possessions of the landlords are named in *italics* with *Roman numerals*.

---

* Acts of Parliament of Scotland, vol iii, pp. 461–467
† Acts of Parliament, vol iv, pp 71–73

Roll of the Landislordis and Baillies.

THE ROLL OF THE NAMES OF THE LANDISLORDIS AND BAILLIES OF LANDIS IN THE HIELANDIS AND ILES, QUHAIR BROKIN MEN HES DUELT AND PRESENTLIE DUELLIS,* 1587

[From the Transactions of the Iona Club, vol 1, 1839, with Notes by the editor, Donald Gregory, Esq, and with additional information by Colonel James A. Robertson]

Landislordis and Baillies

THE DUKE OF LENNOX [1]	The Laird of Marchinstoun [6]	The Laird of Knockhill [12]
The Laird of Buchanane [2]	The Laird of Glennegyis [7]	Hary Schaw of Cambusmoir
The Laird of M'Farlane of the Arroquhar [3]	The Erle of Glencarne [8]	The Laird of Kippanross. [13]
	The Laird of Drumquhassil [9]	The Laird of Burley [14]
The Laird of Luss [4]	The Laird of Kilcreuch [10]	The Laird of Keir [15]
The Laird M'Cawla of Ardincaple [5]	The Tutour of Menteith [11]	The Master of Levingstoun [16]

[1] Ludovick, second Duke of Lennox, whose father, Esme, Lord of Aubigny in France, (son of John, Lord of Aubigny, third son of John third Earl of Lennox, of the Stewarts,) was created by King James VI *Earl* of Lennox, 5th March 1579–80, and *Duke* of Lennox, 5th August 1581

[2] Sir George Buchanan of that ilk, second of that name, and, according to Auchmar, nineteenth Laird of Buchanan The lands of this ancient family lay chiefly in the Highland districts of Menteith and Lennox, in the vicinity of Loch Lomond and Loch Katrine, and are now possessed by the Duke of Montrose

[3] Andrew Macfarlane of that ilk, chief of his ancient clan, descended, in the male line, from *Gilchrist*, a younger son of Alwyn, second Earl of Lennox, of the old family

[4] Humphrey Colquhoun of Luss

[5] Awlay, afterwards Sir Awlay Macawlay of Ardincapill, one of the principal vassals of the Duke of Lennox

[6] Sir Archibald Napier of Merchistoun and Edinbellie father of John Napier of Merchistoun, the celebrated inventor of the Logarithms He possessed considerable lands in the earldoms of Menteith and Lennox, and likewise at Ardownane (or Ardeonaig,) on the south side of Loch Tay, in virtue of his descent from Elizabeth, daughter of Murdac de Menteith, and sister and one of the co-heiresses of Patrick de Menteth of Rusky

[7] John Haldane of Glenagies (now called Gleneagles), descended from Agnes, the other co heiress of the above-mentioned Patrick Menteth of Rusky, through whom he possessed considerable lands in the districts of the Highlands, mentioned in the preceding note

[8] James, seventh Earl of Glencairn Not yet discovered what possessions this nobleman had in the Highlands Perhaps he is only brought here as answerable for his relation, Drumquhassill—(*See next note*) Glencairn was, moreover, connected with the Highlands by marriage, his first wife being eldest daughter (by the second marriage) of Sir Colin Campbell, sixth laird of Glenurchy

[9] John Cunningham of Drumquhassill was served heir to his father, John C of D, in the £5 lands, old extent, of Portnellan, Galbraith, and Tullochan, with the Islands of Loch Lomond, adjacent to the same, in the Dukedom of Lennox, 1613 —(*Special Retours, Co Dunbarten, No 15*)—This ancient family descended from *Andrew* Cunninghame, said to have been a younger son of Sir Robert Cunningham of Kilmaurs, and to have lived in the reign of David II

[10] James Galbraith of Kilcreuch, in the Lennox, is mentioned 1584-5, and Robert Galbraith was laird of Kilcreuch *anno* 1593 —*Registrum Secreti Concilii*

[11] George Graham, tutor or guardian, to John, sixth earl of Menteith, of the Grahams — *Registrum Secreti Concilii*, 1584-5

[12] James Shaw of Knockhill, in Menteith, is mentioned in 1584-5, *Reg Sec Con* , and William Shaw of Knockhill in 1599.—*Compota Thesaurarii Scotiae*

[13] ————Stirling of Kippenross

[14] Sir Michael Balfour of Burleigh, who was superior, if not proprietor, at this time of the lands of Mochaster, &c , in Menteith.

[15] Sir James Stirling of Keir

[16] Alexander, afterwards seventh Lord Livingston This family possessed the lands of Callander and Cornechroinbie in Menteith, with other lands in the Highlands of Perthshire

---

* This and the following ROLL OF CLANS are appended to a long and important Act of Parliament regarding the police of the country, entitled, "For the quieting and keeping in obedience of the disordount subjectis inhabitantis of the Bordouris, Hielandis, and Ilis," but commonly called, from one of its most important provisions, "THE GENERAL BAND," or Bond As this Act of Parliament is very frequently referred to in documents connected with the Highlands, the curious reader is referred to the latest edition of the Acts of the Scottish Parliament (edited by Thomas Thomson, Esq) vol. III pp. 461 to 467, where it is printed entire

The Lord of Down [17]
The Lord Drummond [18]
The Laird of Tullibardin [19]
The Laird of Glenorquhy [20]
The Laird of Lawaris [21]
The Laird of Weyme [22]
The Abbot of Inchaffray [23]
Coline Campbell of Ardbeich [24]
The Laird of Glenlyoun. [25]
The Erle of Athoill [26]
The Laird of Grantullie [27]
The Laird of Strowane-Robertsone [28]

The Laird of Strowane-Murray. [29]
The Laird of Wester Wemyss. [30]
The Laird of Abbotishall [31]
The Laird of Teling [32]
The Laird of Inchmartine. [33]
The Laird of Purie-Fothringhame [34]
The Laird of Moncreiff [35]
The Laird of Balleachane [36]
The Barroun of Fandowie [37]
The Erle of Erroll [38]
The Erle of Gowry [39]
The Laird of Cultybragane [40]

The Lord Ogilvy [41]
The Laird of Clovay. [42]
The Laird of Fintray [43]
The Laird of Edyell [44]
The Erle of Mar [45]
The Master of Elphingstoun [46]
The Erle Huntlie [47]
The Master of Forbes [48]
The Laird of Grant. [49]
Makintosche [50]
The Lord and Tutour of Lovate [51]
Cheisholme of Cummer [52]

[17] James Stewart, first Lord Doune, father of the "bonny Earl of Moray"

[18] Patrick, third Lord Drummond.

[19] Sir John Murray of Tullibardin, in Strathearn This baron also possessed lands in Balquhidder

[20] Duncan, afterwards Sir Duncan Campbell of Glenurchy, seventh laird—one of the most potent of the Highland barons

[21] John, afterwards Sir John, Campbell of Lawers (whose ancestor was a cadet of the family of Glenurchy) He possessed considerable lands both in Breadalbane and Strathearn

[22] James Menzies of that ilk, or of Weym, proprietor of extensive lands in Breadalbane, Strathtay, and Rannoch

[23] James Drummond, Commendator of Inchaffray, and laird of Innerpeffry, possessor also of lands in Balquidder He was brother of Patrick Lord Drummond, and was created, in 1609, Lord Maderty His grandson, William, fourth Lord Maderty, was created Viscount Strathallan in 1686

[24] Brother to Sir Duncan Campbell of Glenurchy His lands lay in the vicinity of Lochearnhead.

[25] Colin Campbell of Glenlyon, descended from the house of Glenurchy.

[26] John, fifth Earl of Atholl, of the Innermeath line.

[27] Sir Thomas Stewart of Grandtully, descended likewise from the house of Innermeath, proprietor of many lands in Strathtay.

[28] Donald Robertson of Strowan, in Atholl

[29] John Murray of Strowan, in Strathearn His daughter was married after this period to *Eoin dubh* Macgregor (afterwards killed at Glenfrune, in 1603), brother to Allaster Macgregor of Glenstray, chief of the Clan Gregor

[30] [31] The editor is unable at present to say who these individuals were, or what was their interest in the Highlands, which the author therefore supplies [There were two families in Fife, *Wemyss of Wester Wemyss*, and *Scott of Abbotshall*, the heads of which are probably meant here The family of Wemyss acquired right to an estate in Atholl, called Kinnaird, by marriage of the heiress of De Inchmartin, Perthshire, which family had married a daughter of John Earl of Atholl, who was beheaded in 1306 The family of Wemyss sold the property of Kinnaird to Stewart of Rosyth, but retained the superiority, and a younger son of Rosyth was the ancestor of the Stewarts of Kinnaird [*Robertson's 'Concise Historical Proofs'*]

[32] Sir David Maxwell of Teling, in Forfarshire He may have possessed lands in the Brae of Angus

[33] Patrick Ogilvie of Inchmartine, proprietor of lands in the south eastern Highlands of Perthshire

[34] Thomas Fothringham of Powrie, also a proprietor in the Brae of Angus

[35] William Moncrieff of that ilk, proprietor of the lands of Culdares and Tenaifhs in Breadalbane, which he afterwards sold to Sir Duncan Campbell of Glenurchy These lands had been possessed by the family of Moncrieff for several centuries

[36] Sir James Stewart of Ballechin, in Athole, descended from a natural son of King James II This family was formerly styled of *Stuiks*

[37] John Macduff, alias Ferguson, Baron of Fandowie, in Atholl, was executed for his accession to Gowrie's Conspiracy, 1600.

[38] Francis, eighth Earl of Errol {This nobleman possessed Logyalmond, part of Inchmartine, and other lands on or near the Highland line

[39] James Ruthven, second Earl of Gowrie, and fifth Lord Ruthven, he possessed lands in Strathardle, and Strathbran, in the south-eastern Highlands of Perthshire. He died in 1588, in his fourteenth year.

[40] Alexander Reidhench of Cultebragan His lands lay in and near Glenleidnoch, in the earldom of Strathern. Edward Reidheuch, fiar of Cultebragan, is frequently mentioned in the records at this period

[41] James, sixth Lord Ogilvy of Airly This nobleman had large possessions in Glen-Isla and other parts of the Brae of Angus

[42] Alexander Ogilvy of Clova was alive in 1557. James Ogilvy was served heir to James Ogilvy of Clova, his father, in the lands of Clova, &c., 1623 The lands of this family lay principally in the Brae of Angus

[43] Sir David Graham of Fintry, Knight, a considerable proprietor in Forfarshire, was alive 1577 This family descended, it is said, from a younger son of the Grahams of Kincardine, afterwards Earls of Montrose

[44] Sir David Lindsay of Edyell, proprietor of Glenesk, and other lands in the Highlands of Forfarshire.

[45] John Erskine, seventh Earl of Mar, proprietor of Braemar, &c

[46] Alexander, afterwards fourth Lord Elphinstone This noble family seem to have possessed Corgarff, in Banffshire, Kildrummy, &c. &c

[47] George, sixth Earl, and afterwards first Marquis of Huntly, Lord of Badenoch and Lochaber

[48] John, afterwards eighth Lord Forbes This family possessed large Highland estates near the sources of the river Don, in Aberdeenshire.

[49] John Grant of Freuchy

[50] Lauchlan Macintosh of Dunauchton, Captain of the Clanchattan.

[51] Simon, eighth Lord Lovat, and Thomas Fraser of Knockie and Strichen, his uncle and guardian

[52] Alexander Chisholm of Strathglass was alive *anno* 1578 John Chisholm of Comer is mentioned *anno* 1613

The Larde of Glengarry.[53]
Mackanyie [54]
The Laird cf Fowlis [55]
The Laird of Balnagown [56]
The Tutour of Cromartie [57]
The Erle of Suthirland [58]
The Laird of Duffus [59]
James Innes of Touchis [60]
The Erle of Caithness.[61]
The Erle Merschall [62]
The Lord Oliphant [63]
The Laird of Boquhowy [64]
The Laird of Dunnybeyth [65]
Macky of Far [66]
Torquill M'Cloyd of Cogoych.[67]
The Laird of Garloch [68]
Makgillichallum of Raarsay.[69]

M'Cloid of the Harrich [70]
M'Kynnoun of Strathodell.[71]
M'Cleud of the Lewes [72]
M'Neill of Barray [73]
M'Kane of Ardnamurchin [74]
Allane M'Kane of Ilandterum.
The Land of Knoydert.[75]
M'Clane of Dowart [76]
The Lard of Ardgowir.[77]
Johnne Stewart of the Appin
M'Coull of Lorne [78]
M'Coull of Roray [79]
The Laird of Lochynnell [80]
The Laird of Caddell [81]
The Laird of Skermourlie, for
     Rauchry [82]

M'Condoquhy of Innerraw [83]
Angus M'Coneil of Dunyveg and
     Glennis
The Laird of Lowip [84]
The Schiref of Bute [85]
The Laird of Camys [86]
Eile of Ergile [87]
Laird cf Auchinbrek [88]
The Laird of Ardkinglass [89]
M'Nauchtane [90]
M'Lauchlane.[91]
The Laird of Lawmont [92]
The Land of Perbrak [93]
The Laird of Duntrune.[94]
Constable of Dundy, Laird of
     Glastry.[95]

---

[53] Donald Macangus [Macranald] of Glengarry, proprietor also in right of his grandmother (Margaret, sister and co heiress of Sir Donald de Insulis of Lochalsh) of the half of the lands of Lochalsh, Lochcarron, and Lochbroom, in Ross shire

[54] Colin Mackenzie of Kintail, whose grandfather had acquired from Dingwall of Kildun, half of the lands of Lochalsh, Lochcarron, and Lochbroom, which Dingwall inherited from his mother Janet, the other co heiress of Sir Donald of Lochalsh.

[55] Robert Munro of Fowlis, said to have been the 15th Baron of that ancient house

[56] Alexander Ross of Balnagown, descended in a direct line from Hugh Ross of Ranches, second son of Hugh, the sixth Earl of Ross, of the old family

[57] John Urquhart of Craigfintry and Culbo, guardian to his grand-nephew Thomas, afterwards Sir Thomas Urquhart of Cromarty

[58] Alexander, eleventh Earl of Sutherland

[59] Alexander Sutherland of Duffus was alive in 1555 William Sutherland of Duffus, probably his son, is mentioned in 1605

[60] The editor has not yet ascertained what lands in the Highlands this individual possessed

[61] George Sinclair, fifth Earl of Caithness

[62] George, fifth Earl Marischall

[63] Lawrence, fourth Lord Oliphant He possessed, among other lands, Berrydale in Caithness, on account of which he appears to be included in this Roll.

[64] Patrick Mowat of Boquhally, a considerable proprietor in Caithness, is mentioned in

1564. Magnus Mowat of Boquhally is mentioned in 1598

[65] William Sinclair of Dunbeath, in Caithness

[66] Hugh Mackay of Farr, father of Donald, first Lord Reay

[67] Torquil Macleod was the eldest son of Roderick Macleod of the Lewis, by that Baron's second marriage with a daughter of Mackenzie of Kintaill During his father's lifetime he held the estate of Cogeache, and was known by that title, but on his father's death he claimed the estates and style of Macleod of Lewis, his title to which was disputed

[68] John Mackenzie of Gairloch

[69] Malcolm Macleod, or Macgillechallum of Rasay, nearest heir male at this time of the Macleods of Lewis, after the descendants of the body of Roderick Macleod of Lewis

[70] William Macleod of Harris, Durvegan, and Glenelg, chief of the *Siol Tormaid*

[71] Lauchlan Mackinnon of Strathwardill in Skye, and of Mishnish in Mull, chief of his ancient tribe

[72] Roderick Macleod of the Lewis, Cogeache and Assint, chief of the *Siol Torcail*

[73] Roderick Macneill of Barra

[74] John Maccoin, or Macian, of Ardnamurchan, chief of an ancient tribe sprung from the family of the Isles

[75] Alexander Macranald of Knoydert, chieftain of his tribe, an ancient branch of the Clanranald

[76] Lauchlan, afterwards Sir Lauchlan Maclean of Dowart, a brave and gallant soldier, as he proved himself by the battle of Glenlivat, in 1594

[77] Ewin Maclean of Ardgoui, representative of an ancient branch of the family of Dowart

[78] Dorgal Macdougal of Dunolly

[79] Allan Macdougal of Raray

[80] Archibald Campbell, second Laird of Lochnell, killed at the battle of Glenlivat, 1594.

[81] John Campbell of Calder or Cadder, frequently written Caddell

[82] Sir Robert Montgomery of Skelmorlie, who seems, at this time, to have possessed the small island of Rachry, or Rachrin, lying near the coast of Antrim.

[83] Dougal Macconachy (Campbell) of Inverraw, head of an ancient sept of the Campbells

[84] Alexander Macallaster of Loupe, in Kintyre

[85] John Stewart Sheriff of Bute

[86] Hector Bannatyne of Kames, in Bute

[87] Archibald, seventh Earl of Argyll, then a minor His principal guardian was John Campbell of Calder

[88] Duncan Campbell of Auchinbreck

[89] Sir James Campbell of Ardkinlass

[90] Malcolm Macnauchtane of Dundaraw

[91] Archibald Maclauchlan of Stralauchlan, or of that ilk

[92] James Lamont of Inveryne, or of that ilk

[93] Colin Campbell of Barbrek

[94] John Campbell of Duntrune

[95] James, afterwards Sir James, Scrymgeour of Dudope, constable of Dundee, and proprietor of the barony of Glasry in Argyleshire, which had been in the possession of this family for many generations

| The Laird of Elanegreg.[96] | The Laird of Coll [98] | M'Fee of Collowsay [100] |
| The Laird of Otter.[97] | Makclayne of Lochbuy [99] | The Lord Hamiltoun [101] |

[96] ———Campbell of Elangreg	[98] Hector Maclean of Coll	[101] Lord John Hamilton, afterwards Marquis
[97] Archibald Campbell younger of Otter is mentioned in 1580	[99] John Maclean of Lochbuy	of Hamilton He is brought in here as proprie-
	[100] Murdoch Macfee of Colonsay	tor of the Isle of Arran

THE ROLL OF THE CLANNIS [IN THE HIELANDIS AND ILES] THAT HES CAPITANES, CHEIFFIS, AND CHIFTANES QUHOME ON THAY DEPEND, OFT TYMES AGANIS THE WILLIS OF THAIR LANDISLORDIS AND OF SUM SPECIALE PERSONIS OF BRANCHIS OF THE SAIDIS CLANNIS, 1587

BUCHANANIS	Stewartis of Athoill, and pairtis adiacent.	Clanlewid of the Lewis
M'Ferlanis, Arroquhar	Clandonoquhy, in Athoill, and pairtis adiacent.	Clanlewyd of Harray.
M'Knabbis.		Clanneil.
Grahmes of Menteth.	Menyessis, in Athoill and Apnadull.	Clankynnoun
Stewartis of Buchquhidder	Clan M'Thomas in Glensche	Clan Ieane [104]
Clangregour	Fergussonis	Clanquhattan
Clanlawren	Spaldingis	Grantis
Campbellis of Lochnell	Makintoscheis, in Athoill.	Frasseris
Campbellis of Innerraw	Clancamroun	Clankanye
Clandowill of Lorne	Claniannald, in Lochquhaber [103]	Clanandreis [105]
Stewartis of Lorne, or of Appin	Clanrannald of Knoydert, Modert, and Glengarry.	Monrois
Clane M'Kane of Avricht.[102]		Murrayis, in Suthirland

| [102] The Clan Eoin, or Macdonalds of Glen-co, whose chief was patronymically styled "*Mac Eoin Abrach.*" | [103] The Macdonalds in the Braes of Loch-aber, commonly called the Macdonalds of Kep-poch | [104] The Clan Eoin of Andnamurchan |
| | | [105] The Rosses of whom Balnagowan was the chief. |

ROLL OF THE BROKEN CLANS IN THE HIGHLANDS AND ISLES," 1594

Oure Soverane Lord and his estaitis in this present Parliament, considering that, nochtwithstanding the sindrie actis maid be his Hienes, and his maist nobill progenitouris, for punischment of the authoris of thift, reiff, oppressioun, and sorning, and masteris and sustenaries of thevis, yet sic hes bene, and presentlie is, the barbarous cruelties and daylie heirschippis of the wickit thevis and lymmaris of the clannis and surenames following, inhabiting the Hielands and Iles ; Thay ar to say —

Clangregour [106]	Clandonochie	Clanronald, in Lochaber.
Clanfarlane.	Clanchattane.[107]	Clanranald, in Knoydert, Modert, and Glengarie
Clanlawren.	Clanchewill.[108]	
Clandowill	Clanchamron.	Clanleyid of the Lewis

| [106] An undesirable precedence seems to be assigned to the Clan Gregor in this Roll | [108] It is doubtful, at present, what tribe is in-dicated by ' *Clan Chewill*' The Clanquhale are named in the year 1392 as followers of the De Athoha family, the ancestors of the Robert-sons of Atholl See 1st vol *Scots Acts Parlia-* | *ment*, p 217, when the whole chieftains of the Clandonachy were forfeited for the two battles in which they had defeated the Lindsays, &c , &c , in 1391 The locality of this tribe seems to have been somewhere in Badenoch or Lochaber |
| [107] It will be observed that the Clanchattan and Macphersons are distinguished from each other in this Roll | | |

* From an Act of Parliament ' for punishment of thift, reiff, oppressioun, and sorning,' vol. iv p 71

Clanlewid of Harriche.	Clankynnoun.	Clanmorgan.[111]
Clandonald, south and north.[109]	Clanneill	Clangun
Clangillane	Clankenyie.	Cheilphale [112]
Clanayioun [110]	Clanandries.	

And als many broken men of the surnames of—

Stewartis, in Athoill, Lorne, and Balquhedder	M'Nabrichis.[113]	M'Inphersonis.[114]
Grahames, in Menteith	Menzeis	Grantis.
Buchannanis.	Fergussonis.	Rossis.
M'Cawlis	Spadingis	Frasseiis
Galbraithis	M'Intoscheis, in Athoill.	Monrois
M'Nabbis	M'Thomas, in Glensche	Neilsonis.[115]
	Ferquharsonis, in Bra of Mar	

And utheris inhabiting the Schirefdomes of Ergyle, Bute, Dunbartane, Striviling, Perth, Forfar, Aberdene, Bamf, Elgin, Forres, Narne, Inuernes, and Cromertie, Stewartries of Stratherne and Menteith, &c

---

[109] The Clandonald South were the Clan Eoin mhor of Isla and Kintyre The Clandonald North were the Clan Huistein of Sky and North Uist

[110] Clan Eoin of Arnamurchan, probably

[111] The Mackays of Strathnaver

[112] A sept of the Mackays, descended from one Paul Macneill Mackay

[113] " M Nabrichis," a contraction probably for *Mac Eoinabrichis*," the Glenco Macdonalds

[114] See Note 107

[115] " *Neilsonis*," the editor conjectures to mean another sept of the Mackays, called by Sir Robert Gordon *Seill Neill*

ROTATION OF THE HIGHLAND CLANS as mentioned in two Acts of Parliament, 1587 and 1594

[The numbers correspond with those given on the Map of the Clans]

1 Buchanan's	22 Clan Ranald of Moydart, Knoydart, Arasaig, Morar, and Glengarry, all Macdonalds
2 M'Farlane's.	
3 M'Nab's	23 ⎱ Clan Leod ⎰ M Leod's of Lewis
4 Graham's of Menteith	24 ⎰ ⎱ M'Leod's of Harris.
5. Stewart's of Balquhidder	25 Clan Neil, or MacNeils
6 Clan Gregor, the M'Gregor's	26 Clan Kinnon, or M'Kinnon's.
7. Clan Lawren, the M'Laren's	27. The Clan Macian, or Macdonald's of Ardnamurchan and Sunnart
8. Campbell's of Lochnell.	
9. Campbell's of Inverawe	28 The Clanchattan, Macphersons, and Mackintoshes.
10 Clan Dougal, M'Dougal's	29 The Grants
11 Stewart's of Appin	30. The Frasers
12. Clan Ian Abrach, or Macdonald's of Glencoe.	31 The Clan Kenzie, or Mackenzie's.
13. Stewart's in Atholl, and parts adjacent.	32 The Clan Anrias, or the Ross's.
14 Clandonachy, or Robertson's of Atholl, and parts adjacent.	33 The Munroes
	34. The Murrays', or Sutherlands'.
15. Menzies's.	35 The Clanquhele, or Shaws of Rothiemurchus
16 Clan M'Thomas, in Glenshee	36 Clan Donald, north and south, Macdonalds'.
17. Fergusson's, in Glenshee	37 The Clan Gillean, or MacLeans
18. Spalding's in Glenshee.	38 The Clan Morgan, or Mackays.
19 M'Intoshe's of Glentilt	39 The Clan Gunn
20. Clan Cameron	40 The Macaulays'.
21 Clan Ranald of Lochaber, or Macdonald's of Keppoch.	41 The Galbraith's
	42 The Farquharson's.

Names of Highland Chiefs and Landlords

IN THE HIGHLANDS AND ISLEL in 1587, contained in the Act of Parliament of that date, and not named in the Roll of the Clans

IV.	Humphrey Colquhoun of Luss.		LII	Alexander Chisholm of that ilk, and Strathglass
XVII.	Earl of Murray, called 'the Bonny Earl'		LXI.	George, fifth Earl of Caithness.
XVIII	Patrick, third Lord Drummond.		LXXXV	John Stewart, Sheriff of Bute.
XX.	Sir Duncan Campbell of Glenurchy.		LXXXVII	Archibald, seventh Earl of Argyll.
XXI	Sir John Campbell of Lawers.		LXXXVIII	Duncan Campbell of Auchenbreck.
XXIV.	Colin Campbell of Ardveck, brother of Sir Duncan Campbell of Glenurchy		LXXXIX.	Sir James Campbell of Ardkinglass
			XC	Malcolm Macnaughtan of Dundaraw
XXV.	Colin Campbell of Glenlyon		XCI	Archibald Maclachlan of Strathlachlan
XXVI	John, fifth Earl of Atholl of the Inner- meath line		XCII	James Lamont of that ilk, Inveryne
			XCIII	Colin Campbell of Barbreck.
XXIX	John Murray of Strowan, in Strathearn		XCIV	John Campbell of Duntroon
XXXIX	James, second Earl of Gowrie, and fifth Lord Ruthven.		XCV	Sir James Scrymgeour of Dudhope and Glassary
XLI	James, sixth Lord Ogilvy of Airly		XCVII	Archibald Campbell of Otter.
XLVII	George, sixth Earl, and first Marquis of Huntly		C	Murdoch Macfie of Colonsay
			CI	John, first Marquis of Hamilton

Strength of the Highland Forces in 1715.

GENERAL WADE gives the following Statement of the Highland Forces in 1715, who fought for King James.

The Islands and clans of the late Lord Seaforth,	3000		Brought forward,	10,620
Macdonalds of Sleat, ...	1000		MacEwen, in the Isle Skye, . . .	150
Macdonalds of Glengarry, .	800		The Chisholms of Strathglass, . .	150
Macdonalds of Moydart, .	800		The M'Phersons, ...	220
Macdonalds of Keppock,	220			
Camerons of Lochiel, .	800		The following clans, he adds, joined *without* having their superiors with them —	
The MacLeods, in all	1000			
The Duke of Gordon's followers, .	1000		The Atholl men, more than one half of whom were Robertsons and Stewarts, . .	2000
Stewarts of Appin, . .	400			
Robertsons of Strowan, .	800		The Breadalbane men, . . .	1000
MacIntoshes and Farquharsons, .	800			
	10,620			14,140

Badges of the Clans.

(From Robertson's *Historical Proofs*)

Suaicheantas* Nan Gael, or, the Badges of the Highland Clans, in Gaelic and English †

Clans	Gaelic	English
Buchanans,	Dearc , braoileag, also Darach	The Bilberry The Oak.
Camerons,	Dearc, Fitheach,	The Crowberry
Campbells,	Garbhag ant sleibh,	Fir Club Moss
Do,	Roid,	Wild Myrtle
Chisholms,	Raineach,	The Fern.
Colquhouns,	Braoileag nan con,	The Dogberry.
Cummings,	Lus mhic Cuiminn,	Cummin Plant
Drummonds,	Lus na Macraidh,	Wild Thyme, the oldest
Do,	Cuilionn,	Holly.
M'Farquhar or Ferguson, and Farquharsons	Ros-grian, Lus-nam-ban-sith,	Little Sunflower, Fox Glove
Forbes and Mackays,	Bealaidh,	Broom,
Frasers,	Iubhar	Yew.
Grants, M'Gregors, M'Kinnons and M'Quarries,	Guithas,	The Scotch Fir
Gordons,	Iadh shlat Eithann,	Ivy.
Grahams,	Buaidh craobh, na laibhreis,	Laurel, the Tree of Victory
Hays,	Uile-ic	Misletoe
MacAulays and Macfarlanes,	Muileag,	Cranberry.
MacDonalds, MacAlastairs, and MacNabs,	Fraoch,	Common Heath
MacDougals,	Fraoch-dearg,	Bell Heath
Mackenzies and MacLeans,	Cuilionn,	Holly.
MacLauchlans,	Faochag,‡	Lesser Periwinkle
Do, Do,	Uinnse,	The Mountain Ash
Macleods, Gunns and Ross,	Aiteann,	Juniper.
MacNauchtans.	Lus Albanach,	The Trailing Azalia.
M'Neills and Lamonts,	Luigh na tri beann,	Trefoil.
Mackays,	Luachair-bhog,	Bull Rushes.
MacPherson, M'Intosh, MacDuffs, MacBeans, Shaws, Farquhar-sons, M'Queens, and many others, as belonging to the Clanchattan,	Craobh aighban,	{Boxwood This is said to be the oldest badge
Do, Do,	Lus na'n Craimsheag Braoilaig,	Red Whortleberry.

* Aodach-suaich eantas, means the national costume or dress complete, with the badge, &c.

† Both Logan, Skene, &c., have been consulted to form this list.

‡ According to Logan.

Clans	Gaelic	English
Menzies's,	Fraoch na Meinearach,	The Menzies Heath
Munro's,	Garbhag na gleann,	Common Club Moss
Murrays, and Sutherlands,	Bealaidh,	Broom
Ogilvies,	Lus Boglus,	Evergreen Alkanet
Oliphants	Luachair,	The Bull Rush
Robertsons,	Dluith Fraoch,	Fine Leaved Heath. This is also said to be the oldest badge.
Do ,	Raineach,	The Fern
Rose's,	Ròs-mairi fiadhaich,	Wild Rosemary
Stewarts,	Darag,	The Oak, also Cluaran, the thistle, the present national badge. That of the Pictish Kings was Rudh (rue), and which is joined with the thistle in the collar of the order.
Urquharts,	Lus-lethn't-samh-raidh,	Wallflower.

War Cries;

OR, RALLYING WORDS OF SOME OF THE CLANS

BUCHANAN'S, 'Clāre Innis,' an island in Loch Lomond

CAMPBELL'S, 'Cruachan,' a well-known mountain in Argyleshire

FARQUHARSON'S, 'Carn na Cuimhne,' 'the Cairn of Remembrance' in Strathdee

FRASER'S, anciently 'Mor-faigh,' or 'Get more,' later 'CastleDownie'

FORBES'S, 'Lonach,' a mountain in Strathdon

Grant's, 'Craig Elachaidh,' or 'Craig Eagalach,' 'the Rock of Alarm,' Strathspey. A portion of the Grants called Clan Chirin have 'Craig Rabhach,' 'the Rock of Warning,' and add, Standsure

MACDONALD'S, 'Fraoch eilean,' 'the Heathy Island'

MACDONALD'S, 'Creig an Fitheach,' 'the Raven's Rock'

MACFARLANES' 'Loch Sloidh,' or 'Loch Sluagh,' the Loch of the People or Host

MACGREGOR'S, 'Ard-coille,' 'the High Wood'

MACINTOSH, 'Loch Moy,' or 'Loch na Maoidh,' the Loch of Threatening,'—a lake near the seat of the Chieftain

M'KENZIE'S, 'Tulach Ard,' a mountain near Castle Donnan, the stronghold of the clan anciently.

M'PHERSON'S, 'Creig dubh Clann Chattan,' 'the Black Craig of the Clan Chattan'

𝕴𝖙𝖎𝖓𝖊𝖗𝖆𝖗𝖞 𝖔𝖋 𝕻𝖗𝖎𝖓𝖈𝖊 𝕮𝖍𝖆𝖗𝖑𝖊𝖘 𝖋𝖗𝖔𝖒 𝖍𝖎𝖘 𝖑𝖆𝖓𝖉𝖎𝖓𝖌 𝖙𝖔 𝕰𝖉𝖎𝖓𝖇𝖚𝖗𝖌𝖍.

THE Prince sailed from Belleisle, in France, on the 12th of July 1745 (*O. S.*), in a small vessel of eighteen guns, called the 'Doutelle,' and landed on the small island of Eriskay, the property of Macdonald of Clanranald, situated between the islands of Barra and South Uist, on the 18th   On the 19th his ship entered the Bay of Lochnanuagh, and anchored near the small village of Forsy, between the shores of Moidart and Arasaig   On the 25th of July the Prince landed on the mainland of Scotland, at a small farm called Borrodaile, Inverness-shire

On the 11th August he sailed to the residence of Macdonald of Kinlochmoidart, about seven miles from Borrodaile   On the 18th he visited the seat of another chieftain of the Macdonald's, in Glenaladale; and, on the following day, proceeded by water to the eastern extremity of Loch Shiel, and on the 19th, the Standard was raised in the vale of Glenfinnan, about forty miles south west of Fort Augustus   The banner was made of red silk, with a white space in the centre, inscribed with the motto, '*Tandem Triumphans*,' and was unfurled by the old Marquis of Tullibardine.   The following morning Charles marched at the head of his men into the country of Lochiel, and took up his residence with that chieftain at Auchnacarrie

On the 21st he removed to Kinlochiel, at the head of Loch Eil, in the Cameron's country   The next day the Prince visited Fassefern, the residence of a younger brother of Lochiel , on the 26th he crossed the river Lochy, and took up his quarters at a small inn at Letterfinlay, on the banks of Loch Lochy

On the 27th he reached Invergarry Castle , next morning he marched in the direction of Corry Arrick, to attack General Cope, who, in the meantime, had retired to Inverness   After traversing the mountainous districts of Badenoch, the Highland army descended, on the second day, into the vale of Atholl   The army encamped at Dalwhinnie, and, on the 30th of August, the Prince arrived at Blair Castle, the residence of the Duke of Atholl.   On the 31st he took up his quarters at the House of Lude, and remained there for two nights. On the 2d of September he proceeded to Nairn House, the seat of Lord Nairn.   On the 3d, the Highland forces were at Auchtergaven.   On the 4th of September the Prince entered Perth, at the head of his army, Lord Nairn riding at his right hand, and Oliphant of Gask on his left, and remained there till the 11th, when he marched to Dunblane, and, on the evening of the 12th, encamped about a mile to the north of that town

On the 13th the army passed the town of Doune, and crossed the ford of Frew, about seven miles above Stirling   That same night the Prince slept at Bannockburn House , on the 14th the army reached Falkirk ; on the 15th, Linlithgow , the 16th and 17th were spent in the march to Edinburgh, and he entered the capital of Scotland on the following day.

𝕴𝖙𝖎𝖓𝖊𝖗𝖆𝖗𝖞 𝖔𝖋 𝕻𝖗𝖎𝖓𝖈𝖊 𝕮𝖍𝖆𝖗𝖑𝖊𝖘 𝖋𝖗𝖔𝖒 𝕰𝖉𝖎𝖓𝖇𝖚𝖗𝖌𝖍 𝖙𝖔 𝕮𝖚𝖑𝖑𝖔𝖉𝖊𝖓.

MARCH OF THE HIGHLAND ARMY, by Captain JAMES STUART of Lord OGILVIE'S Regiment, 1745-46

[Extracted from the Miscellany of the Spalding Club, vol p 277-343]

DATE			PLACE	PAROLE
10th to the 11th October			Holyrood-house	James and Montrose.
11	.	12 .	..	Edward and Canterbury
12	.	13 ..	.	Henry and York
13	...	14 .	...	James and Northumberland
14	...	15 ..		Lewis and Carlisle
16		17 ...	..	Gordon and Galloway
17		18 ..	...	William and Glasgow
18	.	19	.	David and Montrose
19	.	20 .		Taffy and Wales.
20	...	21 ..		Robert and Pembroke
21	.	22	...	Andrew and Scotland
22	.	23 ..	..	Patrick and Ireland.
23	..	24	. .	David and Holyrood-house
24	...	25	.	Daniel and Newcastle
25	...	26 ...	.	John and Skie.
26		27 ..		James and Leith
27	.	28 ..		Henry and York
28	.	29 ..		Charles and Wales
29	.	30 ...	.	William and Aberdeen
30	..	31 ..	Lieth	James and Murray
3		4 November	Tweedale, at Peebles	William and Perth
4		5 .	Broughtoun over Tweed	Charles and York
5	..	6 ..	Erickstain Braefoot	Louis and Aix
6		7 ..	Moffat	John and Strathallan
7	..	8 ..	...	James and Nairn
18	.	19 ..	Carlile	Fortune and Carlile
19	...	20 ...	...	Charles and London
21	.	22 ..	Maclesfield	
22	...	23 ...	. .	Edward and Penrith
23	...	24 ...	Kendal	Charles and York.
24		25 .	...	John and Lancaster
25	.	26 ...	Preston	
27	...	28 ..	.	Henry and Preston
29	...	30 .	Manchester	Henry and York
30	...	1 December	...	St Andrew and Scotland
1	...	2 ...	Macklesfield	James and Newcastle.

B

DATE	PLACE	PAROLE
2d to the 3d December	Macklesfield	Charles and London
3 .. 4	Leik	Henry and Newcastle.
4 . 5	Derby	James and London
5 . 6 .	.	John and Bristol
6 . 7 .	Ashburnham	Richard and Manchester
7	Maclesfield	
8	Stockport	
9 . 10 ..	Manchester	St Taffy and Wales
10	Leigh	
11	Chorley	
12 ... 13 ...	Preston	Edward and Durham
13 . 14	Lancaster	Edward and Lancaster
14 .. 15		Edward and Northumberland
15 16	Kendal	Henry and Peterhead
17 ... 18	Penrith	James and Carlisle
19 ... 20	Carlisle	Charles and France
21	Moffat	
22 23		Drummond and Forth
23 ... 24 ..	Douglass	Ogilvy and Down
24 .. 25	Hamilton	Elcho and Edinburgh
25 . 26	Glasgow	Henry and Hamilton
26 . 27 .		Charles and Edinburgh.
27 ... 28 ...	Glasgow	James and Glasgow
28 . 29	...	Henry and Galloway
29 30		Edward and Edinburgh
30 . 31	.	John and Dover
31 .. 1 January 1746	.	Henry and York
1 .. 2 .	.	Lewis and Paris
2 3 ..		Andrew and Scotland
4 .. 5	Bannockburn	Henry and Essex
5 6 ..	...	Edward and Stirling
6 . 7 ..	.	Charles and Stirling
7 8	..	John and Canterbury
8 9 .	Stirling, St Ringans	Drummond and Perth
10 . 11 .	Stirling	Henry and York
11 .. 12	...	Charles and Athol
12 .. 13 ...	.	Stewart and Gordon
13 ... 14	.	Charles and James
14 . 15 .	..	Wallaceis Oak
15 ... 16 ...	...	Charles and Stirling
16 . 17	Battle of Falkirk	Gordon and Drummond
18	Siege of Stirling	
19, 20, .. 21 ..	.	
22 ...	.	God Speed the Trenches
23 ...	..	William and Glasgow.

		DATE		PLACE	PAROLE
		24	January 1746	Siege of Stirling	Lewis and Inverury
		25	.		Have-at-them at Edinburgh
26	..	27	.		Harry and Essex
27	...	28	...		The Castle of Stirling
28	.	29	.	.	Have-at-them tomorrow
29	..	30	.	.	Charles and Lithgow
30	..	31	..	..	Philip and Peterhead
31	...	I	February		Henry and York
		I	...	Dunblain	
		2	..	Perth	
		3		Coupar of Angus	
		4	.	Cortachy	
		5	...	.	
		6	.	Clova	
		7	...		
		8	.	Cortachy	
		9	.	Clova	
		10	..	.	
		11			
		12	.	Spittal of Glenmuick	
		13	.	Glenmuick Kirk	
		14	...	Colston in Cromarr	
		15	...	Turlan	
		16		Kirk of Reny	
		17	.	Keith	
		18	.	Findrassie	
		19	.	Elgin	
		20	..		
		21	...	..	
		22	...	.	
		23	...		
		24			
		25		Fochabers	
		26		Cullen	
		27	..	..	
		28	.	.	
		I	March		
		2	...	Gordon Castle	
2	...	3		...	Charles and Inverness
3	..	4	...	..	Fitz-James and Aberdeen
4	..	5	.	Fochabers	Spey and Strathbogie
5	.	6	.	..	Charles and Elgin
6	.	7	.		Murray and Portsoy
7	..	8			Perth and Inverness
8	.	9	...	.	Gordon and Elgin

DATE				PLACE	PAROLE
9th to the	10th March			Fochabers	Cromarty and Keith
10	...	11	...	..	Charles and Montrose
11	..	12	. .	. .	Kilmarnock and Strathbogie
12	...	13	...		Nairn and Cullen
13	.	14			Mackintosh and Inverness
14	...	15		Gordon Castle	Pitsligo and Banff
15	.	16	.		Strathallan and Portsoy
16		17	...	.	Ogilvy and Montrose
17	.	18	. .	...	Mareschal and Peterhead
18	...	19	...		Pitsligo and Elgin
		19	.	Diple on the Spey	
		20	..		
		21			
21		22	..	.	Keith and Elcho.
		23		.	
		24			
		25	...	.	
25		2 April		.	Ogilvy and Montrose
2	..	3	..	.	Balmerino and Fochabers
3		7			
7	..	8	..	...	Gordon and Banff
10		11			Charles and Elgin
11		12			Charles and Elgin
		12		Forres	
		13		Nairn	
		14		Culloden	
		15	...	...	
		16		Battle, and retired to Currybroch	
		17	.	Balnahespich by Aviemore, Strathspey	
		18	.	Ruthven of Badenoch	
		19	.	Deeside to Balmurrel	
		20	.	Keppel to Clova	
		21	...	Clova	

N B—Where no Parole is given, it would appear that Lord Ogilvie's Regiment was not at Head Quarters

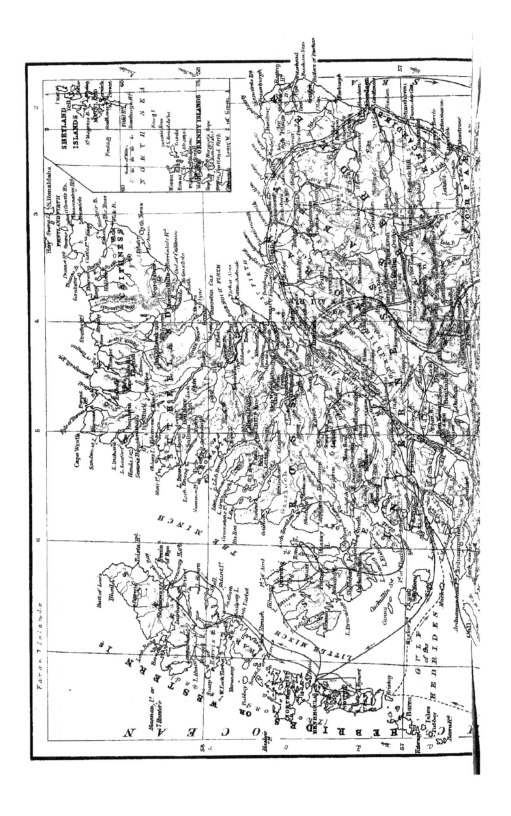

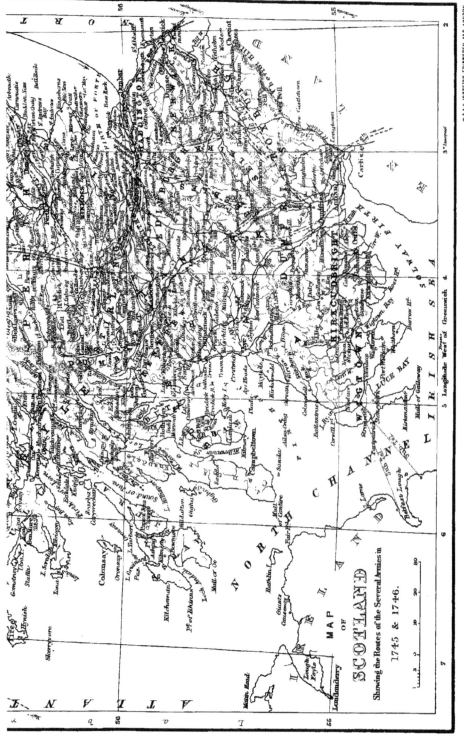

MAP OF SCOTLAND

Showing the Routes of the Several Armies in 1745 & 1746.

The Prince's route before Culloden shewn thus
"   "   "   after   "   "
"   Highland Army's route after Culloden.

General Cope's route shewn thus
"   Wade's   "   "
"   The Duke of Cumberland's route "

W. & A. K. JOHNSTON EDINBURGH AND LONDON

Itinerary of Prince Charles from Culloden to Arasaig.

THE ROUTE OF PRINCE CHARLES, after being defeated by the DUKE OF CUMBERLAND, at Drummossi Muir, near Culloden, 16th April 1746

AFTER the battle, the Prince retired with some few horse, and went by Tordairoch to Gortulaig April 17th, To Invergary Castle, and thence to Glenspean 18th, To Mewboll 19th, Getting no intelligence, he walked to Glen-morrar, thence to Glen-bigsdale, where he waited till he was informed there were no hopes of drawing his troops together 26th, Went on board an open boat in Lochhnanuagh, in the evening, and sailed for the Long Isle 27th, Landed at Rosinish Port, after a violent storm 29th, Set sail for Stornoway 30th, Driven upon the Isle of Scalpay or Glass

May 4th, Landed at Loch Sheffort, and travelled on foot 5th, to Arynish Port, after wandering eighteen hours on the hills in rain 6th, Disappointed of a ship, set sail again and put into the desert Isle of Iffurt 10th, Came again to Glass 11th, Chased by Captain Ferguson, of one of the sloops of war, amongst the rocks of Roudil Port, and afterwards by another ship, but escaped to Loch Escaby 16th, Went to the mountain at Coradale, and staid in that neighbourhood till

June 14th, He sailed to Ouia 18th, Went for Rosinish 20th, In the cleft of a rock at Uishinish Port, thence went to Cehestiella, moving backwards and forwards, till 28th, Embarked in female attire, with Miss Flora M'Donald. 29th, Arrived at Kilbryde, after being fired at by the king's troops at Waternish, and went thence to Kinsburgh 30th, At Portree

July 1st, At Glam 2d, On Nicholson's Rock 3d, In the evening left the Rock, and travelled as a servant to (14th) Elegol, where he embarked at eight that night 5th, Landed at Loch Nevis, and lay three nights in the fields 8th, Closely pursued by the king's troops up Loch Nevis 10th, Arrived in Boradale, and lay in different huts till (15th) Glenalladale came to him 17th, At Corrybenicabir 18th, On the tops of the mountains Scoorug and Fruighven, where the laird of Glenspean conducted him through the guards in the night at this time he was supposed dead 19th, The Prince on the top of the mountain Mamnyncallum 20th, At Corrinangault, all day in sight of small camps, twenty-seven of which were formed, each at half-a-mile's distance from the head of Loch Urin, to the head of Loch Eil, passed several camps, and at last escaped between the sentinels of one of them at the foot of the mountain next to Drymachosey 21st, At Corriscorridill lying all day within cannon shot of two camps, soldiers in sight often. 22d, At Glensheil 23d, On the braes between Glenmoriston and Strathglass 24th, In a cave, where he was joined by the six Glenmoriston men

August 1st, In the woods and shealings of Strathglass, till 7th, set out on his return for Lochiel's country 8th, At Fasnacoil 11th, Among the braes of Glenmoriston 13th, On the brae of Glengary 14th, On the brae of Auchnasual 15th Came to the wood at the foot of Locharkig 19th, Doctor Cameron found him in the wood barefooted, &c Here the Glenmoriston men were dismissed, and staid in this neighbourhood till the 28th, during this time, he was one day nearly taken prisoner by Grant, son to Knokando, but escaped to the top of Mulontagait 28th, Set out for Badenoch to meet Lochiel 29th, Arrived at Corrineuir 30th, Came to Millanuir, where he met Lochiel, who, with his party, were about to fire on him and his guides, not knowing who they were

September 2d, Went to Uiskchilra, two miles farther into Benalder 6th, Went to a hut in the face of the mountain Letternilichk, and remained there till he got intelligence of ships having arrived upon the West coast On the 13th set out for the ships, and came on the morning of the 14th, to Corvoy and before day-light on the 15th got through Glenroy 16th, Came to Achnecairy 17th, Came to Glencambger 19th, Arrived where the ships were. 20th, Set sail in the 'Bellona' of Nantes, and arrived at Roscort, near Morlaix, on the 29th September after narrowly escaping Admiral Lestock's squadron

The Battle of Prestonpans.

ON the 19th of September 1745, Sir John Cope, with his army, lay encamped in a field near Haddington, about sixteen miles from Edinburgh , next morning he resumed his march by the post road, which was left at Huntington, for the low road passing through St Germains and the village of Seton. On reaching the open ground between Seton and Preston, he heard that the Highland Army was on its way to meet him

Sir John had expected that as the Prince and his army had encamped near Edinburgh, the attack would be made from the west and had drawn up his army in a line from north to south, facing west , but when the Highland army appeared on his left, he changed his position, and formed a new line extending from east to west

In the meantime, the Prince drawing his sword, exclaiming as he did so, ' See, gentlemen, I have thrown away the scabbard,' placed himself at the head of his army at Duddingstone, at the base of Arthur's Seat, near which they had encamped, and crossing the river Esk at Musselburgh, proceeded along the post road till they came to Edge Bucklin Brae, there they left the post road, and passing Wallyford on the west side, advanced a good way up Falaside Hill, then turning to the left, bent their course towards Tranent, continuing their march till the two armies were within sight of each other, when the soldiers on both sides shouted vehemently

Near Tranent, the Prince's army halted, and the line of battle was formed facing to the left, within half-a-mile of the King's army Sir John Cope's position was a very strong one naturally, and had been selected with great care; on his left hand he had two enclosures, surrrounded by walls six or seven feet high, between which passed the road to Preston Before him was another enclosure, surrounded by a deep ditch from ten to twelve feet wide, full of water , his left terminated in a morass, and behind was the sea The Highland army finding it impossible to attack the King's army that night, encamped to the east of the village of Tranent, separated from their foes, by what was understood to be, an impassable morass The eastward movement of the Prince's army, again compelled Sir John Cope to change his position, and he re-formed his army nearly on the same ground it had occupied first, extending from north to south, facing east It seemed impossible for the Highland army to attack General Cope, so completely was he entrenched , but at nightfall, Robert Anderson, younger of Whitburgh, a gentleman of property, came to Mr Hepburn of Keith, and informed him that he knew the ground perfectly, and would take on hand to lead the army in safety through the morass without its being seen by the enemy Hepburn recommended that Anderson should go direct to Lord George Murray with the information he had just communicated Lord George was by this time asleep , but, on being roused, he saw the importance of the information, and at once went to inform the Prince, who was asleep, surrounded by many of his chiefs, in a field of peas, which had been cut, but not led

The Highlanders, wrapped in their plaids, were roused from their slumbers with as little noise as possible ; and during the night the whole army passed the morass, near Ringanhead Farm, and formed on the other side, in two lines extending from north to south, facing the Royal army

The night was extremely dark , and when the morning at length dawned, the Highland army was still concealed by a frosty mist. A piquet of dragoons, posted along the side of the morass, was the first to perceive the advance of the Highlanders , they fired their pistols and retreated to the English army, giving the alarm as they went

General Cope was completely taken by surprise , and in the grey light of the early morning mistook the first line of the Highland army, which was within two hundred paces of him, for bushes. This line was led by Lord George Murray, the Duke of Perth being on the right, and consisted of the best armed men, in number about twelve hundred The second line was commanded by Lord Nairne , it consisted of about six hundred men, badly armed, many having nothing but sticks, whilst others had made formidable weapons with scythes fastened to the end of poles The Prince was also with the second line

Lord George did not give the English time to recover from their surprise, but immediately made a rush with the first line of the Highlanders , they, as was their custom, when near the enemy, fired their guns, threw them on the ground, drew their broadswords, and covering their bodies with their shields, in the midst of the smoke rushed upon the foe The Camerons were the first to meet the enemy , and being in front of the royal, artillery, they attacked it with such fury that the men deserted their guns and fled. **The officer in command**

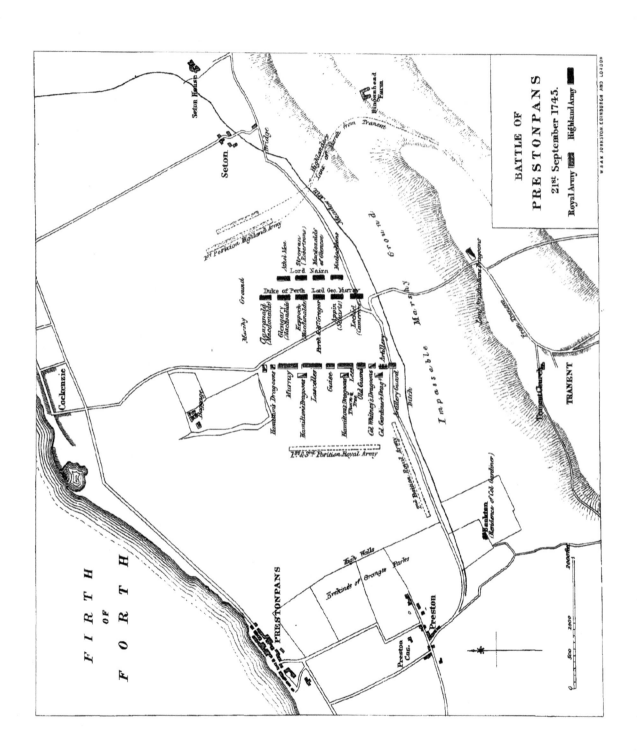

BATTLE OF
PRESTONPANS
21st September 1745.

Royal Army   Highland Army

W. & A.K. JOHNSTON, EDINBURGH AND LONDON

Colonel Whitefoid, when deserted by his men, fired five out of the six guns with his own hand, killing one man, and wounding an officer in Lochiel's regiment The line was then chaiged by cavalry of which the Highlanders had an instinctive fear, as it was an arm they were not accustomed to in their native hills, but they had been directed to strike at the noses of the horses in preference to their riders, the result being, that the wounded animals turned in teiror on those behind them, and spread confusion and dismay in their own ranks, this soon extended to the infantry, who broke and scattered in the wildest disorder

So rapid was the advance of the first line, that although the second was not fifty paces behind it, and advanced at a run, yet the enemy was scattered before it reached the front, the whole affair was over in five minutes The English army fled from the field, throwing away their arms and everything that could encumber their flight, they blocked up the road that led to Preston, and many were killed there in attempting to climb the high walls that surrounded the enclosures at the entrance to the village The M'Giegois, armed with scythes, made sad havoc with the enemy, cutting horsemen nearly in two, and lopping off the legs of horses. The gallant Colonel Gardiner, when deserted by his dragoons, refused to quit the field, and placing himself at the head of a small body of infantry, tried in vain to stem the retreating masses He had been wounded more than once during the brief engagement, and was at length cut down by the Highlanders, within sight of his own house at Bankton, where a monument has since been erected to his memory, a large thorn tree in the middle of the field for long marked the spot where he fell

The English General made his escape from the field, having mounted the 'White Cockade' in his hat, which enabled him to pass through the midst of the Highlandeis on his way to England, where he was the first to carry the news of his own defeat The Prince spent a considerable part of the day on the field of battle, seeing to the protection of the prisoners, and giving directions as to the wounded He passed the night at Pinkie House, about three miles from the scene of his victory

The result of the battle was, that nearly all the standards of the enemy were captured, six pieces of artillery, two howitzers, all the tents, baggage, and the military chest, containing about £2500, besides an immense quantity of arms, of which the Highland army was greatly in want

Of the Royal army only one hundred and seventy of the infantry escaped, about four hundred fell in the battle or in pursuit, and the remainder were taken prisoners The loss of the Highland army was three officers and about forty privates killed, and some seventy wounded

Strength of the two armies, as given in evidence on Sir John Cope's Trial

UNDER SIR JOHN COPE		UNDER PRINCE CHARLES		
Hamilton's Dragoons, .	} 600	Lord Stiathallan's Diagoons,		36
Col Whitneys, „		Clanranald 250		
Col Gardiners, „ .		Glengary 350		
Artillery { 6 1½ Pounders .		Keppoch and Glencoe 450	1st Line	2000
{ 4 Cohoins,		Appin 250		
{ 2 Royals, .		Lochiel 500		
Artillery Guard 100,	} 1400	Perth and M'Giegor 200		
Out Guard 300,		Lord G Murray's Athol Men 350 .	2d Line	1000
Lee's five Companies,		Lord Nairn's Regiment 350		
Guises two „		Menzies of Shian 300 . .		
Lascelles' Regiment,				
Murray's Regiment, .	2000			3036

John Home gives the Highland army, as neaily	.	2400
The Chevalier de Johnstone, as	. .	1800

Note—For the account of the battles of Prestonpans, Falkirk, and Culloden, the Editor is indebted chiefly to the histories of John Home,[*] and the Chevalier de Johnstone,[†] both of whom were present at the battles, and on opposite sides

[*] Lieutenant of the Edinburgh Company of Volunteers.   [†] Aide de-camp to Lord George Murray

The Battle of Falkirk, 17th January 1746.

GENERAL HAWLEY, who succeeded General Cope, arrived in Edinburgh on the 6th of January, to take command of the Royal army, which commenced its march to the west on the 13th, intending to attack the Prince's army at Stirling   The Royal army consisted of twelve regiments of foot, the Glasgow regiment of foot, the Edinburgh Volunteers, and one thousand Argyllshire Highlanders, commanded by Lieutenant-Colonel Campbell, (afterwards Duke of Argyll)   The cavalry consisted of Gardner's, Hamilton's, and Cobham's dragoons.   Seven pieces of cannon completed the army, numbering in all about 8000 men, which consisted of the best troops in the English army, the men, who had fought the battles of Dettingen and Fontenoy   General Hawley seemed rather pleased than otherwise at the defeat of Sir John Cope at Preston, boasting that he (Cope) did not understand such enemies, and that the Highland rabble would never stand a charge of regular troops, if properly led, he seems to have been as arrogant as he was brutal, and made certain of an easy victory whenever he had the good fortune to meet the Prince and his undisciplined army

Arrived at Falkirk on the 16th his army encamped in a field to the west of the town, and, at the invitation of the Countess of Kilmarnock, whose husband was serving under the Prince, General Hawley visited Callander House, situated about half a mile to the south east of Falkirk   There the accomplished Countess seems to have used all her blandishments to make the General neglect his duty, and in this she was so successful, that to her no small share of the victory of Falkirk is due   Meanwhile, on the 16th January, Prince Charles had encamped on Plean Muir, two miles from Stirling, expecting to be attacked by the Royal army, but having ordered a review of all his troops at dawn on the 17th, it was no sooner over than the troops were formed in column, and marched from the field, their destination being kept a profound secret   A small body of horse, under Lord John Drummond, was sent to make a feint along the high road towards Falkirk through Tor Wood (which then extended on both sides of the high road, though it is now confined to the south side of it), while the rest of the Prince's Army went round the south of Tor Wood, and forded the Carron near Dunipace House.   They then marched for the rising ground to the south-west of Falkirk, where Lord John Drummond ultimately took up his position on the left of the second line

The first line consisted of the three Macdonald regiments, Keppoch, Clanranald, and Glengarry, on their left were the Farquharsons, Mackenzies, Mackintoshes, Macphersons, Frasers, Camerons of Lochiel, and on the extreme left the Stuarts of Appin   The second line was composed, on the right, of the three Athol regiments, two of Ogilvie's, two of Gordon's, the Maclauchlan's and the Drummond's, on the left

The reserve, where Prince Charles took up his position, was composed of the Irish piquets, and a small body of horse under Lord Elcho   Lord George Murray commanded the first line, and Lord John Drummond was understood to command the second   The Highland army consisted of 8000 men, and was protected on the right by a morass

About one o'clock, two officers of the Royal army, discovered by means of a telescope, the advanced guard of the Highland army as it emerged from behind Torwood   Lieutenant-Colonel Howard, the second in command, was immediately informed of this, and went off at once to Callander House to inform General Hawley   The General treated the information very lightly, and said 'that the men might put on their accoutrements, but there was no necessity for their being under arms'   The Highland army, marching in two columns, crossed the rising ground to the south of Falkirk, and ascending it from the south, looked right down on the King's army   The Macdonalds were at the head of the first column, gained the top of the hill, when they halted to give time to the remainder of the column to form to their left, and also to allow the second line to form behind them.

The first line, under General Huske, consisted, on the right, of a battalion of the Royals, the regiments of Ligonier, Price, Putney, Cholmondely, and on the left of that of Wolfe.

The second line, on the right, Burrell's, Battereau, Fleming, Munro, and on the left Blakney's.

Irish Piquets Lord Elcho

Prince Charles

Maclachlans Drummonds

Lord John Drummond

Gordons Gordons

Lord Lewis Gordon

Ogilvies Ogilvies

Lord Ogilvy

Lochiel Camerons Appn. Stuarts

Frasers Macphersons

Par quharsons Mackenzies Macdonalds

Macdonalds
Keppoch Clanranald Glengary

Lord Lovat

Lord George Murray

Athol 3 Reg.ts

Morass

Ligonier

Cobham

Ligonier (800)

Hamilton

Ravine

General Husky.

Royals Ligonier Price Wolf

Barrel Battereau Fleming Munro Putney Cholmondely

Buckeny

Howard

Edinr. Voland

Glasgow Militia

PLAN OF THE BATTLE OF FALKIRK

17.th January 1746

Royal Army ◼ Highland Army ◼ Infantry ◼ Cavalry ◣

Map of the Country around Falkirk

Scale of Feet

Falkirk

Camelon

Bantaskin Ho

Grahamston

Callendarho

Falkirk Muir

Prince Charles Well

River Carron

TOR WOOD

Camp
Highland
Army

W. & A.K. JOHNSTON EDINBURGH AND LONDON

The dragoons comprised three regiments, Cobham's, Ligonier's, and Hamilton's, and were commanded by Ligonier Howard's regiment, drawn up behind the right of the second line, formed the reserve, and on their left, the Edinburgh volunteers and the Glasgow militia were stationed, and the Argyleshire Highlanders were left to guard the camp. The accounts vary as to the strength of the Royal Army, some authorities giving it as 8000 men, others at 15,000, but in all probability the two armies were pretty equal as to numbers

In the absence of General Hawley, the commanding officers formed their regiments in front of their encampment, and another messenger was despatched to Callander House, from which the General was at last seen galloping in breathless haste without his hat

The army was at once formed in two lines with a body of reserve The first line consisted of a battalion of the Royals, of the regiments of Wolfe, Cholmondely, Putney, Price, and Ligonier The second line was composed of Burrel's regiment, Blakney's, Munro's, Battereau's and Fleming's Howard's regiment formed the reserve The dragoons were advanced in extended squadrons in front of the infantry, towards its left General Hawley at once ordered his cavalry forward to secure the crest of the hill, before the Highlanders could reach it, the infantry to follow as rapidly as possible. Just as this advance was ordered the day became overcast, and a storm of wind and rain beat directly in the face of the soldiers, who were marching up hill with fixed bayonets The race for the top was gained by the Highlanders, who were formed and ready to receive the dragoons on their arrival, with the great advantage of having the storm of wind and rain from behind, in place of in their faces, the darkness becoming so great, that it was impossible to see to any distance A deep ravine, extending from the top of the hill, ran due north into the plain, getting deeper and wider in its progress This ravine separated the left of the Highland army from the right of the Royal

The dragoons were formed so much to the left and so far in advance, that Lord George Murray, who commanded the Highland army, believed that they were not supported by infantry, and immediately ordered an attack to be made on them, at the very time that General Hawley had ordered Colonel Ligonier, who commanded the cavalry, to advance against the Highlanders, and such was his contempt for them, that this order was given before his infantry had time to form on the crest of the hill Lord George, with his sword drawn and his target on his arm, advanced at the head of the Macdonalds of Keppoch till within a few paces of the dragoons, when he gave the orders to fire, this discharge emptied twenty-four saddles, but still the dragoons rushed forward, breaking their line and trampling many of their opponents under their feet The Highlanders, as usual, threw away their guns, and fought with their swords, and for a time the conflict consisted of a series of single combats, the Highlanders, who had been thrown down in the mêlée, plunged their dirks into the bellies of the horses, whilst others seized their riders by their clothes, pulled them to the ground, despatching them with their pistols or dirks, as there was no room to use their swords.

But this fierce struggle did not last long, the dragoons were vanquished, and retreated in great disorder upon their own infantry, spreading terror through their ranks, which broke and fled down the hill, pursued by the Highlanders, and in the midst of the retreating mass, General Hawley rode with it towards Falkirk

All the English army, however, did not retreat, Burrel's regiment stood fast, and was soon joined by parts of two regiments of the first line (Price's and Ligonier's), this body of resolute men, moved to their left, till they came directly opposite to the Camerons and Stuarts, and began to fire upon them across the ravine The Highlanders kept their ground and returned the fire, but in this mode of warfare they had no chance with the disciplined Royal troops, and after a number had fallen, the Highlanders began to fall back, still keeping the high ground on the side of the ravine This success of the Royal troops put a stop to the pursuit, for the Highlanders hearing so much firing behind them, returned to their former position, expecting to find their second line, but it also had joined in the pursuit, and became a mass of confusion, many thinking that the King's troops had gained a victory, began to retreat, and went off towards the west, whilst the great mass of the English army was retreating towards the east

Farquharson of Monaltry, who had command of the Prince's artillery, had not been able to keep up with the rapid march of the army, was still a mile distant, when he heard the firing, and was shortly afterwards met by some two or three hundred of the Highlanders, retreating from the field   He compelled them to return with him, leaving his artillery behind   Before he arrived, however, Prince Charles and the reserve had advanced to support the Highlanders, and Burrel's regiment, Cobham's dragoons, and the others who had stood with them, were in full retreat towards the camp   General Hawley, before leaving Falkirk with the remains of his army ordered his camp to be set on fire, and then retreated towards Linlithgow, leaving an immense quantity of baggage, provisions, and ammunition, besides seven pieces of cannon, which stuck fast half-way up the hill, and were never brought into action   The battle lasted a very brief time, indeed it was all over in twenty minutes, but by this time darkness had come on, which was greatly increased by the storm which still raged   The confusion was dreadful, no one seemed to know for some time the result of the battle, or where to find either their regiments or officers   Lord Kilmarnock was the first to discover the retreat of the Royal army, but the darkness and disorder were so great, that it was impossible to take advantage of the victory, or collect a sufficient number of troops to complete it, so, the English army, although harassed by as many Highlanders as could be gathered together, made good its retreat to Linlithgow, where it remained all night, after setting fire, either by accident or design, to its beautiful palace, the retreat was continued next day to Edinburgh, where the remains of the royal army arrived about four o'clock in the afternoon   Prince Charles, with his army, remained at Falkirk all night, and returned next day to his former quarters at Bannockburn

Home gives the loss of the Royal army at 300 or 400 men, of officers the loss was very severe—Colonel (Sir Robert) Monro, three Lieutenant-Colonels, Biggar of Monro's regiment, Powell of Cholmondely's, and Whitney of Gardner's, five Captains of Wolfe's, and one Lieutenant, four Captains of Blakney's, and two Lieutenants, beside many wounded.   Johnstone gives the loss of the Royal army at 600 men killed and seven hundred prisoners

Whilst the loss of the Highlanders is stated at 32 officers and men killed, and 120 wounded

The Battle of Culloden.

PRINCE CHARLES, after the victory of Falkirk, at once returned to prosecute the siege of Stirling Castle   On the 30th of January, when fire was at length opened on the Castle, from the battery of three guns, they were almost immediately silenced by the more powerful artillery on the ramparts, and the siege, which had cost the Prince's army so much valuable time, was abandoned.   A paper was now presented to the Prince, signed by Lord George Murray and most of the leading chieftains, urging an immediate retreat to the North; the reason given for this movement being the great desertion that had taken place in their ranks, not from disaffection, but because the Highlanders, as soon as they acquired property of any kind, made it a rule, if at all possible, to return home to deposit their spoil before commencing any new campaign   Thus, there can be little doubt, but that the victory of Falkirk tended in no small degree to the defeat of Culloden   The same day news arrived, that the Duke of Cumberland had reached Edinburgh, and the march to the North, to the grief of the Prince, was commenced next day   The Highland army passed by Dumblane to Crieff, where a separation of the forces took place   one division led by Prince Charles consisting chiefly of the clansmen, marched by the Highland road to Inverness, whilst the other, commanded by Lord George Murray, took the coast road by Montrose and Aberdeen   On the 16th of February, the Prince slept at Moy Castle, about nine miles from Inverness, which, after being joined by the other division of his army, he intended to attack, but Lord Loudon, who commanded the Royal troops there, not having a sufficient force at his command to resist the Highland army, crossed

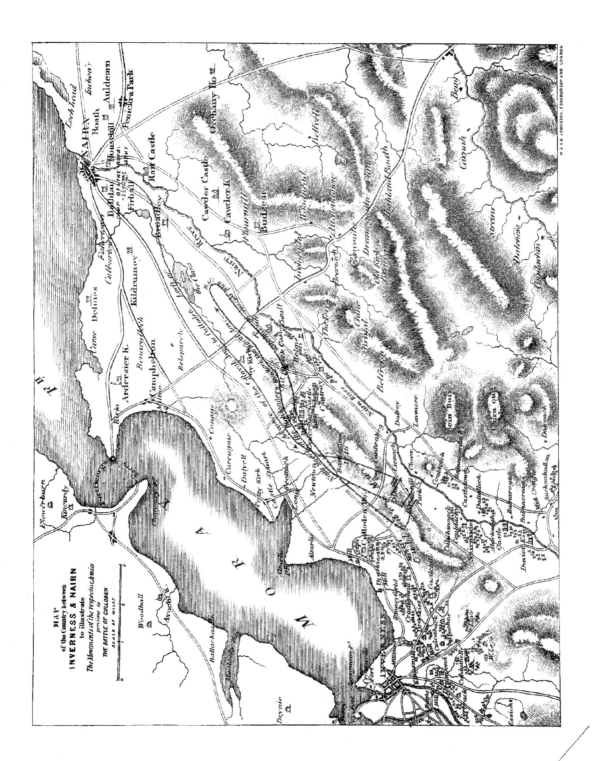

MAP
of the Country between
INVERNESS & NAIRN
to illustrate
The Movements of the respective Armies
previous to
THE BATTLE OF CULLODEN
SCALE OF MILES

the Moray Firth, with all his men, into Ross-shire Two days afterwards, the citadel of Inverness surrendered, and the division under Lord George Murray entered the town on the same day The Duke of Cumberland, who had succeeded General Hawley as commander of the Royal army, arrived in Edinburgh on the 30th of January, commencing his march to the west next morning, he followed the Highland army from Stirling by Perth, through Angus and Aberdeenshire to Aberdeen, where he arrived on the 25th of February, and where he remained till the 8th of April, when he resumed his march to Inverness. On the 10th he reached Banff, on the 11th Cullen, and on the 12th he arrived at the banks of the Spey, which was forded by the Royal army without opposition On the 13th the Duke marched through Elgin to the Muir of Alves, and on the following day entered Nairn The Prince having heard of the arrival of the Royal army at Nairn, collected as many of his scattered forces as were within call, and left Inverness on the 13th of April, marching to Culloden Moor, about four miles north-east of that town, which he had selected for his battle-field He took up his quarters, with his chief officers, at Culloden House, whilst his army passed the night, which was bitterly cold, under arms on the heath, their only food being some biscuits and water In the morning, the Highland army was drawn up in order of battle, it being expected that Cumberland would make an attack that day, but as the 15th was the birth-day of the Duke, it was held as a holiday, and given up to feasting and mirth

The Prince called a Council of War to consider what was best to be done in the present position of their affairs, at which Lord George Murray proposed a night attack on the Royal army at Nairn As the project entirely met with the views of the Prince, it was after some discussion agreed to In the evening the Highlanders were aroused from their slumbers, and formed into two columns, the first being led by Lord George Murray, and the second by the Prince in person In silence and darkness the Highlanders commenced their march to Nairn, twelve miles distant, across fields, with scarcely any roads, and such as were could not be seen The best disciplined troops could not have preserved order in such a march, and with such difficulties to contend with, and as might have been anticipated, some from hunger began to scatter in search of food, and others lagged behind from sheer exhaustion, worst of all, the leading column had outstripped the second, and it became necessary to call a halt to enable it to join, so that a simultaneous attack might be made A message was despatched to the rear, to intimate to the Prince the necessity for this halt, but the Prince insisted on Lord George advancing at once on the enemy's camp, and intimated that he would follow to support him as rapidly as possible It had been arranged that the attack would be made at two o'clock in the morning, but when that hour arrived, the leading column was still four miles from Nairn The beat of a drum was heard in the Royal camp, and it was now evident that the night surprise was hopeless (Home states that the Duke's spies had informed him of every stage of the night attack) Under these circumstances, Lord George Murray ordered a retreat, at which the Prince, when made aware of it, was very indignant, but consoled himself with the hope that the two armies would soon meet

Famishing with hunger, and worn out with their night's march, the exhausted Highlanders arrived about five o'clock in the morning on their camping ground on Culloden Moor Many of the men went off at once in search of food and rest, several had got the length of Inverness, when all that were within hearing were recalled by the discharge of a cannon, and the pipes playing the 'Gathering' of the various clans, but many were beyond recall, and did not return in time to take part in the battle The Prince repaired to Culloden House, when, with difficulty, some bread and whisky were procured for him

Worn out with his long march, he laid himself down to rest, which, however, was of short duration, for in little more than two hours he was awoke to be informed that the enemy's cavalry was not more than two miles distant, and was followed by the whole army The Prince immediately mounted his horse, and, accompanied by Lord George Murray, the Duke of Perth, and Lord John Drummond, rode to the site selected for the battle-field, which was about a mile to the west of the ground occupied by the army on the previous day The ground was uneven and marshy, the water in many places reaching to the knees of the Highlanders, but for this very reason it formed the better protection from the enemy's cavalry The right of the position was protected by a strong stone wall, which surrounded an enclosure extending nearly to the water of Nairn, and the left extended in the direction of Culloden House   The Highland army was drawn up in the following order —the right wing, commanded by Lord George Murray, consisted of the following clans—Atholl, Lochiel, Appin, Cluny   The centre, under Lord John Drummond—Lovat, M'Intosh, Farquharson, M'Leod   The left, under the Duke of Perth—Maclean, Clanranald, Keppoch, and Glengairy   On the right, immediately behind the first line, under General Stapleton, were posted the French and Irish piquets, and Fitz-James' Horse   Behind the centre of the first line, the Prince, with a small body of Horse Guards, took up his position , behind the first line on the left were Lord John Drummond's regiment, the Perthshire squadron of horse, and a few hussars   The second line consisted of Colonel Roy Stuart's regiment, Lord Lewis Gordon's, and Glenbucket's men, and Kilmarnock's Guards   Behind the second line was the *corps de reserve*, consisting of the Duke of Perth and Lord Ogilvy's men   Four guns were placed on the extremity of each wing, and four in the centre   The Duke of Cumberland seems to have marched from Nairn, keeping as much as possible in the order of battle, and when within cannon-shot of the Highland army, were drawn up in the following order —The right wing, under Major-General Bland, consisted of Kingston's horse and the Royal regiment   The centre, under the Earl of Albemarle, Cholmon-dely's and Price's regiments, the Scotch fusileers, and Munro's regiments   The left, under Lord Ancrum, Burrel's regiment and Kerr's and Cobham s dragoons   The second line, under Major-General Husk, Fleming's, Bligh's, Sempil's, Legonier's, and Wolfe's regiments   The third line, under Brigadier Mordaunt, on the right and left Kingston's horse (which were afterwards moved to front right wing) Howard's, Pultney's, Butteran's, and Blackney's regiments   Two guns were placed between each regiment in the first line, and three on each wing of the second   The Duke is represented as being in *front* of Cholmondely's regiment

The Highlanders, although in a very exhausted condition, were far from being dismayed by the formidable appearance of the Royal army, and were all impatience to be attack ,led to the the battle, however, was com-menced by the artillery on both sides, which kept up a continuous fire for nearly an hour , that of the Prince's army was badly served, and did little execution, the shot passing generally over the heads of the enemy   On the other hand, the Royal artillery was well served, and told severely on the ranks of the Highlanders, who, having suffered severely, at last lost patience, and the M'Intoshes, who had never before been engaged, broke their ranks, and rushed forward   Lord George Murray, on the right, seeing that his men could be restrained no longer, ordered them to advance, which they did with a shout   In spite of the shower of grape-shot which met their advance, the clansmen pressed on and broke through Monro's and Burrel's regiments, capturing two cannon   Not content with this, the advance was continued till it was checked by the second line, which was drawn up as if to repel cavalry—the first rank kneeling, the second stooping over the first, and the third standing upright   Such a destructive fire was poured into the advancing clansmen that they halted, and the few that were able retreated in confusion , but so determined had been the attack, and so vigorously had it been repulsed, that the Highlanders were found, when the strife was over, heaped on each other, three and four deep   The M'Intoshes, and some of the clans of the centre, although suffering from a galling fire, succeeded also in piercing the enemy's line, but were repulsed by the steady fire of the reserve, and were also compelled to retreat   The left wing, consisting of the three Macdonald regiments, took no part in the fight   They had been accus-tomed to have the right of the field of battle ever since Bannockburn, and felt insulted at being placed on the left for the first time   In vain did the Duke of Perth entreat them to advance , he told them that by their courage they might convert the left into the point of honour, and if they would but charge, he would be proud to adopt the surname of Macdonald   In vain did Keppoch, their gallant captain, exclaim, ' My God ! have the children of my tribe forsaken me ?' he rushed forward, waving them on with his sword, but he was followed by only a few of his immediate kinsmen, and had advanced but a short way when he fell mortally wounded   But still the Macdonalds kept their ground, and they are represented as hewing in their rage with their swords the heather at their feet, and falling in their ranks from the enemy's fire, which they did not return   It is thought, that had the whole line charged at once, it would have gone hard with the Royal army, which, as it was, was

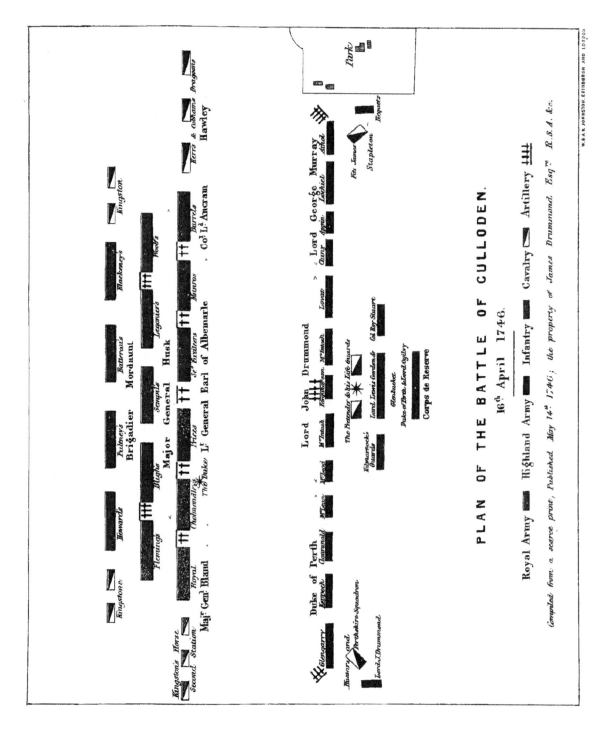

PLAN OF THE BATTLE OF CULLODEN.

16th April 1746.

Royal Army ▬▬ Highland Army ▬▬ Infantry ▬▬ Cavalry ◣ Artillery ⚏

Compiled from a scarce print, Published May 14th 1746; the property of James Drummond, Esqr. R.S.A. &c.

W. & A.K. JOHNSTON, EDINBURGH AND LONDON.

severely shaken   In the meantime, it had completed its victory by the Campbells breaking down the walls of the enclosure which protected the right of the Prince's army, through which Kerr's and Cobham's dragoons, led by Hawley, poured, attacking the broken line in flank   The retreat now became general, but the Highlanders, especially those of the second line, kept well together, and left the field with pipes playing and colours flying   The Irish and French piquets did good service, by protecting, by a well-directed fire, the retreat of the clansmen   Prince Charles was not so completely overpowered by this destruction of all his hopes as to make him loose his usual courage, on the contrary, he urged those around him to make one more effort to retrieve the fortune of the day, and insisted on leading personally his shattered army once more against the enemy   His friends saw that this could only lead to the total destruction of his faithful followers, and at length O'Sullivan siezed the bridle of his horse, and forced him from the field   When we consider the condition and number of the combatants, the wonder is, not that Prince Charles lost the battle, but that the Highland army was able to offer the resistance that it did

The Duke's army had marched northward by the coast road, attended by a fleet of transports carrying provisions, and all the material required by a well-appointed army   The Royal troops were well fed, clothed, and paid, and had every comfort that an army on the march can have, whilst, on the other hand, the Highlanders had had no pay for months, they had no tents or protection of any kind from the piercing cold and rain, they had no commissariat, and many of them were literally starving for want of food, add to this, that the men had just returned from a midnight march of sixteen miles, and that the Royal army on the field numbered more than two to one, and it will be seen how little Cumberland had to boast of his victory.

Of the barbarities committed after the battle, this is not the place to speak, but one cannot help contrasting the behaviour of the ' Cousins in the hour of victory

Cumberland superintending, with evident satisfaction, the murder in cold blood of the unfortunate prisoners and wounded that had fallen into his hands (many of them gentlemen of high standing and of undoubted courage), nay, even 'insulting the slain '   On the other hand, Prince Charles remaining on the fields he and his gallant followers had won, to protect the prisoners and wounded, and to soothe, as much as possible, the distress of the vanquished   The Prince never forgot that his enemies were still his countrymen, the Duke forgot that they were human beings

As might be expected, the accounts vary as to the number of the respective armies, but Patullo, muster-master of the Prince's army, gives the number on the roll as 8000 men, but adds that 3000 were absent, then the three regiments of Macdonalds, who took no part in the fight, numbered 1150, reducing the number to 3850

On the other hand, the Duke's army consisted of upwards of 9000 of the best disciplined and appointed troops in the British Army

In the battle, the total number killed seems to have amounted to 1200, and the loss appears to have been about equally divided

Anno Decimo Nono

Georgii II. Regis.

An Act for the more effectual disarming the Highlands in Scotland, *and for more effectually securing the Peace of the said Highlands; and for restraining the Use of the Highland Dress, and for further indemnifying such Persons as have acted in defence of his Majesty's Person and Government, during the unnatural Rebellion, and for indemnifying the Judges and other Officers of the Court of Justiciary in* Scotland, *for not performing the Northern Circuit in* May, *One thousand seven hundred and forty six, and for obliging the Masters and Teachers of Private Schools in* Scotland, *and Chaplains, Tutors and Governors of Children or Youth, to take the Oaths to His Majesty, His Heirs, or Successors, and to register the same*

Preamble reciting the Acts, 1 *Geo.* I

WHEREAS by an Act made in the First Year of the Reign of His late Majesty King *George* the First, of Glorious Memory, intituled, *An Act for the more effectual securing the Peace of the Highlands in* Scotland, it was enacted, That from and after the First Day of *November*, which was in the Year of our Lord One thousand seven hundred and sixteen, it should not be lawful for any Person or Persons (except such Persons as are therein mentioned and described) within the Shire of *Dunbartain*, on the North Side of the Water of *Leven, Stirling* on the North Side of the River of *Forth, Perth, Kincardin, Aberdeen, Inverness, Nairn, Cromarty, Argyle, Forfar, Banff, Sutherland, Caithness, Elgine*, and *Ross*, to have in his or their Custody, Use, or Bear, Broad Sword or Target, Poignard, Whinger, or Durk, Side Pistol, Gun, or other warlike Weapon, otherwise than in the said Act was directed, under certain Penalties appointed by the said Act, which Act having by Experience been found not sufficient to attain the Ends therein proposed, was further enforced by

10 & 11 *Geo* I an Act made in the Eleventh Year of the Reign of His late Majesty, intituled, *An Act for more effectual disarming the Highlands in that Part of* Great Britain *called* Scotland, *and for the better securing the Peace and Quiet of that Part of the Kingdom* And whereas the said Act of the Eleventh Year of His late Majesty being, so far as it related to the disarming the Highlands, to continue in Force only during the Term of Seven Years, and from thence to the End of the next Session of Parliament, is now expired And whereas many Persons within the said Bounds and Shires still continue possessed of great Quantities of Arms, and there, with a great Number of such Persons, have lately raised and carried on a most audacious and wicked Rebellion against His Majesty, in favour of a Popish Pretender, and in Prosecution thereof did, in a traiterous and hostile Manner, march into the Southern Parts of this Kingdom, took Possession of several Towns, raised Contributions upon the Country, and committed many other Disorders, to the Terror and great Loss of His Majesty's faithful Subjects, until, by the Blessing of God on His Majesty's Arms, they were subdued Now, for preventing Rebellion, and traiterous Attempts in Time to come, and the other Mischiefs arising from the Possession or Use of Arms, by lawless, wicked, and disaffected Persons inhabiting within the said several Shires and Bounds, be it enacted by the King's most Excellent Majesty, by and with the Advice and Consent of the Lords Spiritual and Temporal, and Commons, in this present Parliament assembled, and by the Authority of the same, That from and after the First Day of *August*, One thousand seven hundred and forty six, it shall be lawful for the

Lord Lieu- tenants, &c respective Lords Lieutenants of the several Shires above recited, and for such other Person or

Persons as His Majesty, His Heirs, or Successors shall, by His or Their Sign Manual, from time to time, think fit, to authorise and appoint in that Behalf, to issue, or cause to be issued out, Letters of Summons in His Majesty's Name, and under his or their respective Hands and Seals, directed to such Persons within the said several Shires and Bounds, as he or they, from time to time, shall think fit, thereby commanding and requiring all and every Person and Persons therein named, or inhabiting within the particular Limits therein described, to bring in and deliver up, at a certain Day, in such Summons to be prefixed, and at a certain Place therein to be mentioned, all and singular his and their Arms and warlike Weapons, unto such Lord Lieutenant, or other Person or Persons appointed by His Majesty, His Heirs, or Successors, in that Behalf, as aforesaid, for the Use of His Majesty, His Heirs, or successors, and to be disposed of in such Manner as His Majesty, His Heirs, or Successors shall appoint, and if any Person or Persons, in such Summons mentioned by Name, or inhabiting within the Limits therein described, shall, by the Oaths of One or more credible Witness or Witnesses, be convicted of having or bearing any Arms, or warlike Weapons, after the Day prefixed in such Summons, before any One or more of His Majesty's Justices of the Peace for the Shire or Stewartry where such Offender or Offenders shall reside, or be apprehended, or before the Judge Ordinary, or such other Person or Persons as His Majesty, His Heirs, or Successors shall appoint, in Manner herein after directed, every such Person or Persons so convicted shall forfeit the Sum of Fifteen Pounds Sterling, and shall be committed to Prison until payment of the said Sum, and if any Person or Persons, convicted as aforesaid, shall refuse or neglect to make Payment of the foresaid Sum of Fifteen Pounds Sterling, within the Space of One Calendar Month from the Date of such Conviction, it shall and may be lawful to any One or more of His Majesty's Justices of the Peace, or to the Judge Ordinary of the Place where such Offender or Offenders is or are imprisoned, in case he or they shall judge such Offender or Offenders fit to serve His Majesty as a Soldier or Soldiers, to cause him or them to be delivered over (as they are hereby impowered and required to do) to such Officer or Officers belonging to the Forces of His Majesty, His Heirs, or Successors, who shall be appointed from time to time to receive such Men, to serve as Soldiers in any of his Majesty's Forces in *America*, for which Purpose the respective Officers, who shall receive such Men, shall then cause the Articles of War against Mutiny and Desertion to be read to him or them in the Presence of such Justices of the Peace, or Judge Ordinary, who shall so deliver over such Men, who shall cause an Entry or Memorial thereof to be made, together with the Names of the Persons so delivered over, with a Certificate thereof in Writing, under his or their Hands, to be delivered to the Officers appointed to receive such Men, and from and after reading of the said Articles of War, every Person so delivered over to such Officer, to serve as a Soldier as aforesaid, shall be deemed a listed Soldier to all Intents and Purposes, and shall be subject to the Discipline of War, and in case of Desertion, shall be punished as a Deserter, and in case such Offender or Offenders shall not be judged fit to serve his Majesty as aforesaid, then he or they shall be imprisoned for the space of Six Calendar Months, and also until he or they shall give sufficient Security for his or their good Behaviour for the Space of Two Years from the giving thereof

And be it further enacted by the Authority aforesaid, That all Persons summoned to deliver up their Arms as aforesaid, who shall, from and after the Time in such Summons prefixed, hide or conceal any Arms, or other warlike Weapons, in any Dwelling-house, Barn, Out-house, Office, or any other House, or in the Fields, or any other Place whatsoever, and all Persons who shall be accessary or privy to the hiding or concealing of such Arms, and shall be thereof convicted by the Oaths of One or more credible Witness or Witnesses, before any One or more of His Majesty's Justices of the Peace, Judge Ordinary, or other Person or Persons authorized by His Majesty in Manner above mentioned shall be liable to be fined by the said Justices of the Peace, Judge

Margin notes:
to issue Summons for delivering up of Arms

The Penalty

On Non payment of the Penalty, the Persons, if fit, are to serve as Soldiers in *America*

Articles of War to be read to them, and entry thereof to be made, &c

If unfit, to be imprisoned for Six Months, and find Bail

Concealing, &c of Arms,

Ordinary, or other Person authorised by His Majesty, before whom he or they shall be convicted

the Penalty
according to their Discretion, in any Sum not exceeding One hundred Pounds Sterling, nor under the Sum of fifteen Pounds Sterling, of lawful Money of *Great Britain*, and shall be committed

On Non pay ment the Per sons, if fit, to be delivered over to serve as Soldiers in *America,*
to Prison until Payment , and if the Person so convicted, being a Man, shall refuse or neglect to pay the Fine so imposed, within the Space of One Calendar Month from the Date of the said Conviction, he shall, in case he be judged by any One or more Justice or Justices of the Peace, or the Judge Ordinary of the Place were such Offender is imprisoned, fit to serve His Majesty as a Soldier, be delivered over to serve as a Soldier in His Majesty's Forces in *America*, in the

if not fit, to be imprisoned for Six Months, and find Bail
Manner before directed, with respect to Persons convicted of having or bearing of Arms , and in case such Offender shall not be judged fit to serve His Majesty as aforesaid, then he shall be imprisoned for the Space of Six Calendar Months, and also until he shall give sufficient Security for his good Behaviour, for the Space of Two Years from the giving thereof , and if the Person

Penalty on Women, if convicted
convicted shall be a Woman, she shall, over and above the foresaid Fine, and Imprisonment till payment, suffer Imprisonment for the Space of Six Calendar Months, within the *Tolbooth* of the Head Burgh of the Shire or Stewartry within which she is convicted

And be it further enacted by the Authority aforesaid, That if, after the Day appointed by

Arms hidden in any House, &c, the Tenant to be deemed and and suffer as the Concealer, &c
any Summons for the delivering up of Arms in pursuance of this Act, any Arms or warlike Weapons, shall be found hidden or concealed in any Dwelling-house, Barn, Out-house, Office, or any other House whatsoever, being the Residence or Habitation of or belonging to any of the Persons summoned to deliver up Arms as aforesaid, the Tenant or Possessor of such Dwelling-house, or of the Dwelling-house to which such Barn, Office, or Out-house belongs, being thereof convicted in Manner above mentioned shall be deemed and taken to be the Haver and Concealer of such Arms, and being thereof convicted in Manner above mentioned, shall suffer the Penalties hereby above enacted against Concealers of Arms, unless such Tenant or Possessor, in whose House, Barn, Out-house, Office, or other House by them possessed, such Arms shall be found concealed, do give Evidence, by his or her making Oath, or otherwise to the Satisfaction of the said Justices of the Peace, Judge Ordinary, or other Person authorized by His Majesty, before whom he or she shall be tried, that such Arms were so concealed and hid without his or her Knowledge, Privity, or Connivance

Second Of fence Trans portation
And be it further enacted by the Authority aforesaid, That if any Person who shall have been convicted of any of the above Offences, of bearing, hiding, or concealing Arms, contrary to the Provisions in this Act, shall thereafter presume to commit the like Offence a second Time, that he or she being thereof convicted before any Court of Justiciary, or at the Circuit Courts, shall be liable to be transported to any of His Majesty's Plantations beyond the Seas, there to remain for the Space of Seven Years

Officers to be appointed by His Majesty
And for the more effectual Execution of this present Act, be it further enacted by the Authority aforesaid, That it shall be lawful to His Majesty, His Heirs, or Successors, by His or Their Sign Manual from time to time, to authorize and appoint such Persons as he or they shall think proper, to execute all the Powers and Authorities by this Act given to One or more Justice or Justices of the Peace, or to the Judge Ordinary, within their respective Jurisdictions, as to the apprehending, trying, and convicting such Person or Persons who shall be summoned to deliver up their Arms, in pursuance of this Act

What shall be a sufficient Summons, and legal Notice
And to the end that every Person or Persons named or concerned in such Summons, may have due Notice thereof, and to prevent all Questions concerning the Legality of such Notice, it is hereby further enacted by the Authority aforesaid, That such Summons, notwithstanding the Generality thereof, be deemed sufficient, if it express the Person or Persons that are commanded to deliver up their Weapons, or the Parishes, or the Lands, Limits, and Boundings of the respective

Territories and Places, whereof the Inhabitants are to be disarmed as aforesaid, and that it shall be a sufficient and legal Execution or Notice of the said Summons, if it is affixed on the Door of the Parish Church or Parish Churches of the several Parishes within which the Lands (the Inhabitants whereof are to be disarmed) do lie on any *Sunday*, between the Hours of Ten in the Forenoon, and Two in the Afternoon, Four Days at least before the Day prefixed for the delivering up of the Arms, and on the Market Cross of the Head Burgh of the Shire or Stewartry within which the said Lands lie, Eight Days before the Day appointed for the said Delivery of the Arms, and in case the Person or Persons employed to affix the said Summons on the Doors of the several Parish Churches, or any of them shall be interrupted, prevented, or forcibly hindered, from affixing the said Summons on the Doors of the said Churches, or any of them, upon Oath thereof made before any of His Majesty's Justices of the Peace, the Summons affixed on the Market Cross of the said Head Burgh of the Shire or Stewartry as aforesaid, shall be deemed and taken to be a sufficient Notice to all the Persons commanded thereby to deliver up their Arms, within the true Intent and Meaning, and for the Purposes of this Act

    And to the end that there may be sufficient Evidence of the Execution, or Notice given of the Summons for disarming the several Persons and Districts, as aforesaid, be it further enacted by the Authority aforesaid, That upon the elapsing of the said several Days to be prefixed for the delivering up Arms, the Person or Persons employed to fix the Summons, as above mentioned, on the Market Cross of the Head Burghs of any Shire or Stewartry, shall, before any One of His Majesty's Justices of the Peace for the said Shire or Stewartry, make Oath, that he or they did truly execute and give Notice of the same by affixing it as aforesaid, and the Person or Persons employed to affix the said Summons on the Doors of the Parish Church or Parish Churches, shall make Oath in the same Manner, and to the same Effect or otherwise shall swear that he or they were interrupted, prevented, or forcibly hindered from affixing the said Summons as aforesaid, which Oaths, together with Copies or Duplicates of the Summons, to which they severally relate, shall be delivered to the Sheriff or Stewart Clerk of the several Shires or Stewartries within which the Persons intended to be disarmed do live or reside, who shall enter the same in Books, which he and they is and are hereby required to keep for that Purpose, and the said Books in which the Entries are so made, or Extracts out of the same, under the Hand of the Sheriff or Steward Clerk, shall be deemed and taken to be full and complete Evidence of the Execution of the Summons, in order to the Conviction of the Persons who shall neglect or refuse to comply with the same

    And be it further enacted by the Authority aforesaid, That if any such Sheriff or Steward Clerk neglect or refuse to make such Entry as is above mentioned, or shall refuse to exhibit the Books containing such Entries, or to give Extracts of the same, being thereto required by any Person or Persons who shall carry on any Prosecutions in pursuance of this Act, the Clerk so neglecting or refusing shall forfeit his Office, and shall likewise be fined in the Sum of Fifty Pounds Sterling, to be recovered upon a summary Complaint before the Court of Session, for the Use of His Majesty, His Heirs, or Successors

    And be it further enacted by the Authority aforesaid, That it shall and may be lawful to and for the Lord Lieutenant of any of the Shires aforesaid, or the Person or Persons authorized by His Majesty, His Heirs, or Successors, as aforesaid, to summon the Person or Persons aforesaid to deliver up his or their Arms, in manner above mentioned, or to and for any One Justice of the Peace of the respective Shires above mentioned, or to the Judge Ordinary within their respective Jurisdictions or to such Person or Persons as shall be authorized by His Majesty, His Heirs, or Successors, for trying Offences against this Act, to authorize and appoint such Person or Persons

Margin notes:

Evidence of Notice given of the Summons to be made on Oath

Oath, with Duplicates of the Summons, to be delivered to the Sheriff, &c and to be entered, then Evidence to be good

Sheriff not making Entry, &c

the Penalty

Lord Lieutenants, &c to appoint Persons to summon,

C

*and appre-
hend, &c
such as shall
be found with
Arms*

as they shall think fit, to apprehend all such Person or Persons as may be found within the Limits foresaid, having or wearing any Arms, or warlike Weapons, contrary to Law, and forthwith to carry him or them to some sure Prison, in order to their being proceeded against according to Law

And be it further enacted by the Authority aforesaid, That it shall and may be lawful to and for His Majesty, His Heirs, and Successors, by Warrant under His or Their Royal Sign Manual, and also to and for the Lord Lieutenant of any of the Shires aforesaid, or the Person or Persons authorized by His Majesty, to summon the Person or Persons aforesaid to deliver up their Arms, or any One or more Justices of the Peace, by Warrant under his or their Hands, to authorize and

*Search may
be made for
Arms, by
Day or Night*

appoint any Person or Persons to enter into any House or Houses, within the Limits aforesaid, either by Day or by Night, and there to search for and to seize all such Arms as shall be found contrary to the Direction of this Act

*Search by
Night to be
made in
Presence of a
Constable, &c
In case of
Opposition,*

Provided, That if the above mentioned Search shall be made in the Night-Time, that is to say, between Sun setting and Sun rising, it shall be made in the Presence of a Constable, or of some Person particularly to be named for that Purpose in the Warrant for such Search, and if any Persons, to the Number of Five or more, shall at any Time assemble together to obstruct the Execution of any Part of this Act, it shall and may be lawful to and for every Lord Lieutenant, Deputy Lieutenant, or Justice of the Peace where such Assembly shall be, and also to and for every Peace Officer within any such Shire, Stewartry, City, Burgh, or Place where such Assembly shall be, and likewise to and for all and every such other Person or Persons, as by His Majesty, His Heirs, or Successors, shall be authorized and appointed in that Behalf as aforesaid, to require

*the Aid of the
King's Forces
to be called.*

the Aid and Assistance of the Forces of His Majesty, His Heirs, or Successors, by applying to the Officer commanding the said Forces (who is hereby authorized, impowered, and commanded to give such Aid and Assistance accordingly) to suppress such unlawful Assembly, in order to the putting this Act in due Execution, and also to seize, apprehend, and disarm, and they are hereby

*Offenders to
be carried
before a
Justice*

required to seize, apprehend, and disarm such Persons so assembled together, and forthwith to carry the Persons so apprehended before One or more of His Majesty's Justices of the Peace of the Shire or Place where such Persons shall be so apprehended, in order to their being proceeded against, for such their Offences, according to Law, and if the persons so unlawfully assembled, or any of them, or any other Person or Persons summoned to deliver up his or their Arms in pursuance of this Act, shall happen to be killed, maimed or wounded in the dispersing, seizing, and apprehending, or in the endeavouring to disperse, seize, or apprehend, by reason of their resisting the Persons endeavouring to disperse, seize, and apprehend them; then all and every such Lord Lieutenant, Deputy Lieutenant, Justice or Justices of the Peace, or any Peace Officer or Officers, and all and every Person or Persons, authorized and appointed by His Majesty, His Heirs, or Successors, in that Behalf, as aforesaid, and all Persons aiding and assisting to him, them, or any of them,

*Indemnifica
tion against
Persons killed
resisting*

shall be freed, discharged, and indemnified, as well against the King's Majesty, His Heirs, and Successors, as against all and every other person and persons of, for, or concerning the killing, maiming, or wounding any such Person or Persons so unlawfully assembled, that shall be so killed, maimed, or wounded as aforesaid

*Defendant to
be allowed the
Indemnity,
and his Ex-
penses*

And be it further enacted by the Authority aforesaid, That if any Action, Civil or Criminal, shall be brought before any Court whatsoever, against any Person or Persons for what he or they shall lawfully do in pursuance or Execution of this Act, such Court shall allow the Defendant the Benefit of the Discharge and Indemnity above provided, and shall further decern the Pursuer to pay to the Defender the full and real Expences that he shall be put to by such Action or Prosecution

Provided nevertheless, and be it enacted by the Authority aforesaid, That no Peers of this Realm, nor their Sons, nor any Members of Parliament, nor any Person or Persons, who, by the Act above recited of the First Year of His late Majesty, were allowed to have or carry Arms, shall by virtue of this Act be liable to be summoned to deliver up their Arms, or warlike Weapons, nor shall this Act, or the above recited Act, be construed to extend to exclude or hinder any Person, whom His Majesty, His Heirs, or Successors, by Licence under His or Their Sign Manual, shall permit to wear Arms, or who shall be licenced to wear Arms, by any Writing or Writings under the Hand and Seal, or Hands and Seals of any Person or Persons authorized by His Majesty, His Heirs, or Successors, or give such Licence from keeping, bearing, or wearing such Arms, and warlike Weapons, as in such Licence or Licences shall for that Purpose be particularly specified *[margin: Persons exempted from delivering up their Arms]*

And to the end that no Persons may be discouraged from delivering up their Arms, from the Apprehension of the Penalties and Forfeitures which they may have incurred, through their neglecting to comply with the Directions of the said Act of the First Year of His late Majesty's Reign, be it further enacted by the Authority aforesaid, That from and after the Time of affixing any such Summons as aforesaid, no Person or Persons residing within the Bounds therein mentioned, shall be sued or prosecuted for his or their having, or having had, bearing, or having borne Arms, at any Time before the several Days to be prefixed or limited by Summons as aforesaid, for the respective Persons and Districts to deliver up their Arms, but if any Person or Persons shall refuse or neglect to deliver up their Arms in Obedience to such Summons as aforesaid, or shall afterwards be found in Arms, he and they shall be liable to the Penalties and Forfeitures of the Statute above recited, as well as to the Penalties of this present Act *[margin: Act 1st Geo I / None to be sued for having had Arms before the Time limited for delivering them up / Penalty on not delivering up Arms]*

And be it further enacted by the Authority aforesaid, That One Moiety of the Penalties imposed by this Act with respect to which no other Provision is made, shall be to the Informer or Informers, and the Other Moiety shall be at the Disposal of the Justices of the Peace, Judge Ordinary, or other Person authorized by His Majesty as aforesaid, before whom such Conviction shall happen, provided the same be applied towards the Expence incurred in the Execution of this Act *[margin: Disposal of Forfeitures]*

And be it further enacted by the Authority aforesaid, That the above Provisions in this Act shall continue in Force for Seven Years, and from thence to the End of the next Session of Parliament, and no longer *[margin: The above Provisions to be in force for 7 Years]*

And be it further enacted by the Authority aforesaid, That from and after the First Day of *August*, One thousand seven hundred and forty seven, no Man or Boy, within that Part of *Great Britain* called *Scotland*, other than such as shall be employed as Officers and Soldiers in His Majesty's Forces, shall, on any Pretence whatsoever, wear or put on the Clothes commonly called *Highland Clothes* (that is to say) the Plaid, Philebeg, or little Kilt, Trowse, Shoulder Belts, or any Part whatsoever of what peculiarly belongs to the Highland Garb, and that no Tartan, or party-coloured Plaid or Stuff shall be used for Great Coats, or for Upper Coats; and if any such Person shall presume after the said First Day of *August*, to wear or put on the aforesaid Garments, or any Part of them, every such Person so offending, being convicted thereof by the Oath of One or more credible Witness or Witnesses before any Court of Justiciary, or any One or more Justices of the Peace for the Shire or Stewartry, or Judge Ordinary of the Place where such Offence shall be committed, shall suffer Imprisonment, without Bail, during the Space of Six Months, and no longer, and being convicted for a second Offence before a Court of Justiciary, or at the Circuits, shall be liable to be transported to any of His Majesty's Plantations beyond the Seas, there to remain for the Space of Seven Years *[margin: None but the Army to wear the Highland Clothes / The Penalty]*

And whereas by an Act made in this Session of Parliament, intituled, *An Act to indemnify such Persons as have acted in Defence of His Majesty's Person and Government, and for the Pre-* *[margin: Act 19 Geo. II]* servation of the publick Peace of this Kingdom during the Time of the present unnatural Rebellion, and Sheriffs and others who have suffered Escapes, occasioned thereby, from vexatious Suits and Prosecutions, it is enacted, That all personal Actions and Suits, Indictments, Informations, and all Molestations, Prosecutions, and Proceedings whatsoever, and Judgments thereupon, if any be, for or by reason of any Matter or Thing advised, commanded, appointed, or done during the Rebellion, until the Thirtieth Day of *April*, in the Year of our Lord One thousand seven hundred and forty six, in order to suppress the said unnatural Rebellion, or for the Preservation of the publick Peace, or for the Service of Safety to the Government, shall be discharged and made void. And whereas it is also reasonable, that Acts done for the publick Service, since the said Thirtieth Day of *April*, though not justifiable by the strict Forms of Law, should be justified by Act of Parliament, be it

All Actions, for Matters done for the Service of the Government, to be void, &c

enacted by the Authority aforesaid, That all personal Actions and Suits, Indictments and Informations, which have been or shall be commenced or prosecuted, and all Molestations, Prosecutions, and Proceedings whatsoever, and Judgments thereupon, if any be, for or by reason of any Act, Matter, or Thing advised, commanded, appointed, or done before the Twenty fifth Day of *July*, in the Year of our Lord One thousand seven hundred and forty six, in order to suppress the said unnatural Rebellion, or for the Preservation of the publick Peace, or for the Safety or Service of the Government, shall be discharged and made void, and that every Person, by whom any such Act, Matter, or Thing shall have been so advised, commanded, appointed or done for the Purposes aforesaid or any of them, before the said Five and twentieth Day of *July*, shall be freed, acquitted, and indemnified, as well against the King's Majesty, His Heirs, and Successors, as against all and every other Person and Persons, and that if any Action or Suit hath been or shall be commenced

England

or prosecuted, within that Part of *Great Britain* called *England*, against any Person for any such Act, Matter, or Thing so advised, commanded appointed, or done for the Purposes aforesaid, or any

General Issue

of them, before the said Twenty fifth Day of *July*, he or she may plead the General Issue, and give this Act and the special Matter in Evidence, and if the Plaintiff or Plaintiffs shall become nonsuit, or forbear further Prosecution, or suffer Discontinuance, or if a Verdict pass against such Plaintiff

Double Costs

or Plaintiffs, the Defendant or Defendants shall recover his, her, or their Double Costs, for which he, she, or they shall have the like Remedy, as in Cases where Costs by Law are given to Defendants, and if such Action or Suit hath been or shall be commenced or prosecuted in that Part of *Great*

Scotland

Britain called *Scotland*, the Court, before whom such Action or Suit hath been or shall be commenced or prosecuted, shall allow to the Defender the Benefit of the Discharge and Indemnity

Full Costs

above provided, and shall further decern the Pursuer to pay to the Defender the full and real Expences that he or she shall be put to by such Action or Suit.

Act 6 *Anna*

And whereas by an Act passed in the Sixth Year of Her late Majesty Queen *Anne*, intituled, *An Act for rendering the Union of the Two Kingdoms more entire and complete*, it is, among other Things, enacted, That Circuit Courts shall be holden in that Part of the United Kingdom called *Scotland*, in Manner, and at the Places mentioned in the said Act. And whereas by the late unnatural Rebellion, the Course of Justice in *Scotland* has been so interrupted, as rendered it impracticable to give up and transmit Presentments, in such due Time as Prosecutions might thereupon commence, before the Northern Circuit, to be holden in *May* this present Year, whereby there appeared a Necessity of superseding the said Circuit, be it therefore enacted by the

Judges indemnified for not performing the Circuit Courts

Authority aforesaid, That the Judges of the Court of Justiciary, and all and every other Person and Persons therein concerned, are hereby indemnified for their not performing the said Circuit, as by the forecited Act they were obliged to do, any thing in the same Act, or in any other Law or Statute to the contrary notwithstanding.

And whereas a Doubt hath arisen with respect to the Shire of *Dumbartain*, what Part thereof was intended to be disarmed by the First recited Act made in the First Year of His late Majesty

King *George*, and intended to be carried into further Execution by the present Act, be it enacted by the Authority aforesaid, That such Parts of the said Shire of *Dunbartain* as ly upon the East, West, and North Sides of *Lochlomond*, to the Northward of that Point where the Water of *Leven* runs from *Lochlomond*, are and were intended to be disarmed by the aforesaid Act and are comprehended and subject to the Directions of this Act

(margin: Parts of Dunbartain to be disarmed)

And whereas it is of great Importance to prevent the rising Generation being educated in disaffected or rebellious Principles, and although sufficient Provision is already made by Law for the due Regulation of the Teachers in the Four Universities, and in the publick Schools authorized by Law in the Royal Burghs and Country Parishes in *Scotland*, it is further necessary, That all Persons who take upon them to officiate as Masters or Teachers in Private Schools, in that Part of *Great Britain* called *Scotland*, should give Evidence of their good Affection to His Majesty's Person and Government, be it therefore enacted by the Authority aforesaid, That from and after the First Day of *November*, in the Year of our Lord One thousand seven hundred and forty six, it shall not be Lawful for any Person in Scotland to keep a Private School for Teaching *English, Latin, Greek*, or any Part of Literature, or to officiate as a Master or Teacher in such School, or any School for Literature, other than those in the Universities, or Established in the respective Royal Burghs by Publick Authority, or the Parochial Schools settled according to Law, or the Schools maintained by the Society in *Scotland* for propagating Christian Knowledge, or by the General Assemblies of the Church of *Scotland*, or Committees thereof, upon the Bounty granted by His Majesty, until the Situation and Description of such Private Schools be first entered and registered in a Book, which shall be provided and kept for that Purpose by the Clerks of the several Shires, Stewartries, and Burghs in *Scotland*, together with a Certificate from the proper Officer, of every such Master and Teacher having qualified himself, by taking the Oaths appointed by Law to be taken by Persons in Offices of publick Trust in *Scotland*, and every such Master and Teacher of a Private School shall be obliged, and is hereby required, as often as Prayers shall be said in such School, to pray, or cause to be prayed for, in express words, His Majesty, His Heirs, and Successors, by Name, and for all the Royal Family, and if any Person shall, from and after the said First Day of *November*, presume to enter upon, or exercise the Function or Office of a Master or Teacher of any such Private School as shall not have been registered in Manner herein directed, or without having first qualified himself, and caused the Certificate to be registered as above mentioned, or in case he shall neglect to pray for His Majesty by Name, and all the Royal Family, or to cause them to be prayed for as herein directed, or in case he shall resort to, or attend Divine Worship in any Episcopal Meeting-house not allowed by the Law every Person so offending in any of the Premisses, being thereof lawfully convicted before any Two or more of the Justices of the Peace, or before any other Judge competent of the Place summarily, shall, for the first Offence, suffer Imprisonment for the Space of Six Months, and for the Second, or any subsequent Offence, being thereof lawfully convicted before the Court Justiciary, or in any of the Circuit Courts, shall be adjudged to be transported, and accordingly shall be transported to some of his Majesty's Plantations in *America* for Life, and in case any Person adjudged to be so transported shall return into, or be found in *Great Britain*, then every such Person shall suffer Imprisonment for Life

(margin: Situation of Private &c Schools to be registered, with a Certificate of the Master having qualified himself)

(margin: His Majesty, &c to be prayed for by Name)

(margin: Masters not to resort to Episcopal unlicensed Meeting-houses The Penalty)

And be it further enacted by the Authority aforesaid, That if any Parent or Guardian shall put a Child or Children under his care to any Private School that shall not be registered according to the Directions of this Act, or whereof the principal Master or Teacher shall not have registered the Certificate of his having qualified himself as herein directed, every such Parent or Guardian so offending, and being thereof lawfully convicted before any Two or more Justices of Peace, or before any other Judge competent of the Place summarily, shall, for the First Offence be liable to suffer

(margin: Parents, &c sending Children to unregistered Schools, &c)

the Penalty   Imprisonment by the Space of Three Months, and for the Second, or any subsequent Offence, being thereof lawfully convicted before the Court of Justiciary, or in any of the Circuit Courts, shall suffer Imprisonment for the Space of Two Years from the Date of such Conviction

And whereas by an Act passed in the Parliament of *Scotland*, in the Year of our Lord One thousand six hundred and ninety three, all Chaplains in Families, and Governours and Teachers of Children and Youth, were obliged to take the Oaths of Allegiance and Assurance therein directed, and there may be some Doubt, whether by the Laws, as they stand at present, they are obliged to take the Oaths appointed to be taken by Persons in Offices of publick Trust in *Scotland* Therefore be it enacted by the Authority aforesaid, That from and after the First Day of *November*, in the Year of our Lord One thousand seven hundred and forty six, no Person shall exercise the

Chaplains, &c.   Employment, Function, or Service of a Chaplain, in any Family in that Part of *Great Britain* called
in Families,   *Scotland*, or of a Governor, Tutor, or Teacher of any Child, Children, or Youth, residing in *Scotland*,
to take the
Oaths   or in Parts beyond the Seas, without first qualifying himself, by taking the Oaths, appointed by

Certificates to   Law to be taken by Persons in Offices of publick Trust, and causing a Certificate of his having
be registered   done so to be entered or registered in a Book to be kept for that Purpose by the Clerks of the Shires, Stewartries, or Burghs in *Scotland*, where such Persons shall reside, or in case of any such Governor, Tutor, or Teacher of any such Child, Children, or Youth, acting in Parts beyond the Seas, then in a Book to be kept for that Purpose by the Clerk of the Shire, Stewartry, or Burgh where the Parent or Guardian of such Child, Children, or Youth shall reside   And if any Person, from and after the said First Day of *November*, shall presume to exercise the Employment, Function, or Service of Chaplain, in any Family in *Scotland*, or of a Governor or Teacher of Children or Youth, as aforesaid, without having taken the said Oaths, and caused the Certificate of his having duly taken the same, to be registered, as is above directed, every Person so offending, being thereof lawfully convicted before any Two or more Justices of Peace, or before any other Judge Competent of the Place summarily, shall for the First Offence, suffer Imprisonment by the Space

The Penalty   of Six Months, and for the Second, or any subsequent Offence, being thereof lawfully convicted before the Court of Justiciary, or in any of the Circuit Courts, shall be adjudged to be banished from *Great Britain* for the Space of seven Years

Provided always, That it shall be lawful for every Chaplain, Schoolmaster, Governour, Tutor, or Teacher of Youth who is of the Communion of the Church of Scotland, instead of the Oath of Abjuration appointed by Law to be taken by Persons in Offices Civil or Military, to take the Oath

Oath ap-   directed to be taken by Preachers and Expectants in Divinity of the established Church of
pointed for
Chaplains,   *Scotland*, by an Act passed in the Fifth Year of the Reign of King *George*, the First, intituled, *An*
&c. of the   *Act for making more effectual the Laws appointing the Oaths for Security of the Government to be*
Church of
Scotland   *taken by Ministers and Preachers in Churches and Meeting-houses in Scotland*, and a Certificate of
Act 5 Geo I   his having taken that Oath shall, to all Intents and Purposes, be as valid and effectual as the Certificate of his having taken the Oath of Abjuration above mentioned, and he shall be as much deemed to have qualified himself according to Law, as if he had taken the Abjuration appointed to be taken by Persons in Civil Offices

Persons keep-   And be it further enacted, That from and after the said First Day of *November*, no Person
ing Chaplains,
&c. who have   within *Scotland* shall keep or entertain any Person or Chaplain in any Family, or as Governor,
not qualified,   Tutor, or Teacher of any Child, Children, or Youth, unless the Certificate of such Person's having taken the Oaths to His Majesty be duly registered in Manner above directed, and if any Person shall keep or entertain a Chaplain in his Family, or a Governor, Tutor, or Teacher of any Child, Children, or Youth under his Care, without the Certificate of such Chaplain, Governor, Tutor, or Teacher's having respectively qualified himself, by taking the Oaths to His Majesty, being duly registered in Manner above mentioned, every such Person so offending, being thereof lawfully

convicted before any Two or more of His Majesty's Justices of Peace, or before any other Judge competent, shall, for the First Offence, suffer Imprisonment by the Space of Six Months, and for the Second, or any subsequent Offence, being thereof lawfully convicted before the Court of Justiciary, or in any of the Circuit Courts in *Scotland*, shall suffer Imprisonment by the Space of Two Years

the Penalty

And for the better preventing any private Schools from being held or maintained, or any Chaplain in any Family, or any Governor, Tutor, or Teacher of any Children or Youth, from being employed or entertained contrary to the Directions of this Act, be it further enacted, That the Sheriffs of Shires, and Stewarts of Stewartries, and Magistrates of Burghs in Scotland, shall be obliged, and are hereby required, from time to time, to make diligent Enquiry within their respective Jurisdictions, concerning any Offences that shall be committed against this Act, and cause the same, being the First Offence, to be prosecuted before themselves, and in case of a Second, or subsequent Offence, to give Notice thereof, and of the Evidence for proving the same, to his Majesty's Advocate for the Time being, who is hereby required to prosecute such Second or subsequent Offences before the Court of Justiciary, or at the Circuit Courts

Sheriffs, &c. to enquire into Offences against this Act, &c

F I N I S.

Now Ready, SECOND EDITION, in Demy Quarto, Price, Full Bound Cloth, 7s. 6d.

THE
HISTORICAL GEOGRAPHY
OF THE
CLANS OF SCOTLAND.

BY

T. B. JOHNSTON, F.R.G.S. F.R.S.E. & F.S.A.S.,

AND

COLONEL JAMES A. ROBERTSON, F.S.A.S.

CONTENTS.

MAP OF SCOTLAND DIVIDED INTO CLANS (Large folding Map, Coloured, and mounted on Cloth).
PREFACE.
EXPLANATORY REMARKS ON THE MAP.
ROLL OF THE LANDISLORDIS AND BAILLIES.
ROTATION OF THE HIGHLAND CLANS AS GIVEN IN TWO ACTS OF PARLIAMENT, DATED 1587 AND 1594.
NAMES OF HIGHLAND CHIEFS AND LANDLORDS CONTAINED IN THE ACT OF PARLIAMENT 1587, NOT NAMED IN THE ROLL OF THE CLANS.
STRENGTH OF THE HIGHLAND FORCES IN 1715.
BADGES OF THE CLANS.
WAR CRIES OF THE CLANS.
ITINERARY OF PRINCE CHARLES FROM HIS LANDING TO EDINBURGH.

ITINERARY OF PRINCE CHARLES FROM EDINBURGH TO CULLODEN.
ITINERARY OF PRINCE CHARLES FROM CULLODEN TO ARASAIG.
MAP OF THE VARIOUS ROUTES (TWO PAGES Coloured).
ACCOUNT OF THE BATTLE OF PRESTONPANS.
PLAN OF THE BATTLE (Coloured).
ACCOUNT OF THE BATTLE OF FALKIRK.
PLAN OF THE BATTLE (Coloured).
ACCOUNT OF THE BATTLE OF CULLODEN.
MAP OF THE DISTRICT, WITH LINE OF MARCH OF THE TWO ARMIES.
PLAN OF THE BATTLE (Coloured).
ACT OF PARLIAMENT, DATED 1746, FOR DISARMING THE HIGHLANDS, AND RESTRAINING THE USE OF THE HIGHLAND DRESS.

The Work, with the Map mounted on Cloth, on Roller varnished, can be had for Two Shillings extra.

EXTRACTS FROM REVIEWS.

'The Map bears evidence of careful preparation, and the Editor acknowledges the assistance of Dr William Skene, who is known for eminent services to Highland archæology.'—*Athenæum.*

'Every Highland gentleman should at once provide himself with a copy of this graceful volume, so well-fitted to add ornament to a drawing-room. Indeed, every lady and gentleman with a Highland name, ought to be speedily quite familiar with its contents. We cordially commend the book to every student of the history of Scotland.'—*Courant.*

'This is a valuable contribution to the history of the Scottish Highlands, and a delightful work for enthusiastic Highlanders. Great pains have been taken to make the Map as accurate as possible. It may lay claim to be the most complete, as well as the most correct, ever published.'—*Daily Review.*

'It would appear that there is a strong desire for information as to the limits and positions occupied by the Clans of Scotland; and the publishers of this volume, to supply this demand, first started with a Map, here given—a very handsome one too—showing the geographical position of the Clans in Scotland. After that came certain interesting additions—now happily matters of history, merely curious, but which will be useful, and, no doubt, interesting, to our Scottish readers.' —*Publishers' Circular.*

'This is in every way, an admirable work. There is no authentic map of the districts occupied by the Highland Clans at any particular date, and the authors supply us with one which

has for its basis the Acts of Parliament of 1587 and 1594. The map is invaluable to the historical student. Antiquarians and students of Scottish history will seldom fall upon so many curious and interesting particulars as this most interesting tract supplies, presented in so limited a space. The narratives of the battles are concise and impartial, and are yet full of spirit.'—*Glasgow Herald.*

'Geography is the right eye of history. Strange to say, while the history of continental contests, like the Peninsular war and the campaign of 1815, have been fully illustrated by maps and plans, the histories of our own country are almost destitute of illustrations of this sort. We, therefore, hail with peculiar satisfaction, a work which purposes to supply this deficiency in regard to the last great effort to replace the Stewart family on the throne of Great Britain—a theme of undying interest to Scotchmen in every quarter of the world. The Map has been constructed with great labour and care, and is the first properly authenticated and accurate document of the kind that has been given to the public. The work is tastefully and carefully got up, the plans of the battles are well executed, and on the whole correct.'—*North British Daily Mail.*

'The Historical Geography of the Clans of Scotland is a volume of very considerable interest to historians generally, and to Scotchmen in particular. Mr T. B. Johnston and Colonel J. A. Robertson must be congratulated on having done their work exceedingly well.'— *The Evening Standard.*

'It may be expected that not only all the St

Andrew's, Caledonian, Gaelic, Burns, and other Scottish Societies, but all those of Scotch birth or descent, whose names begin with *Mac* and end with *Son*, will take very kindly to a publication of unexampled accuracy, which tells them, in a few words, a great deal about their families.'— *The Press*, Philadelphia, U.S.

'In the historical, and one or two other departments of literature, the importance of a thoroughly good map can scarcely be overstated. With much judgment, advantage has been taken of the publication of the Clan Map to republish a variety of interesting particulars as to the Highland Clans, which are not now easy of access to ordinary readers. We congratulate Messrs Johnston on this addition to their well-earned reputation. The map is executed with the elegance, clearness, and finish which distinguish all the geographical works issuing from their establishment, and the work is, in other respects, exceedingly well got up.'—*The Crieff Journal.*

'The most useful of all companions to any History of Scotland, or of the Highlands, or, indeed, to any history of our country, that has been prepared, is the volume now before us, entitled "The Historical Geography of the Clans of Scotland." It is therefore a volume which every student in history, and, notably, every Scotsman ought to possess. It is long since we saw so truly interesting and useful a contribution to historical literature as this book in every way is. It overflows with curious and suggestive matter, and leaves nothing to be desired.'—*Reliquary Quarterly Journal.*

W. & A. K. JOHNSTON,
GEOGRAPHERS, ENGRAVERS, AND PRINTERS TO THE QUEEN,
EDINBURGH AND 74 STRAND, LONDON.

1873.

CPSIA information can be obtained
at www.ICGtesting.com
Printed in the USA
BVOW07s2009090817

491642BV00005B/123/P